DISCARD

LOOKING AHEAD TO MARRIAGE

marriage

By

A Team of Daughters of St. Paul

looking ahead to

GLORY TO GOD   PEACE TO MEN

ST. PAUL EDITIONS

NIHIL OBSTAT:
  ROBERT J. BANKS
    Diocesan Censor Deputatus

IMPRIMATUR:
  ✠ RICHARD CARDINAL CUSHING
    Archbishop of Boston

September 30, 1969

Library of Congress Catalog Card Number: 74—92550

Printed by the *Daughters of St. Paul*
50 St. Paul's Avenue, Jamaica Plain,
Boston, Mass. 02130   .

LOOKING AHEAD
TO MARRIAGE

Marriage is the most common way of life, the path which the majority of God's sons are called to tread. For this reason young men and women are presented with this volume which aims to help them make their marriage a *happy* one.

Taine says: "It is quite a common thing for newlyweds to contemplate each other for three weeks, to love each other for three months, to quarrel for three years, to tolerate each other for thirty years, and then to see their own children go through the same process." This volume, therefore, does not present "Cinderella situations" but tries to stick to that objective norm of *reality,* always taking into account Christian faith and the supernatural.

The *choice of a partner, engagement, the wedding day, newlyweds, in-laws, family harmony, the budget, fidelity, children, divorce, birth control*—this is but a sketch of the panorama which unfolds in this comprehensive marriage course.

Building on the doctrine of marriage as reconfirmed by Vatican II, (numbers 47 to 52 of the Pastoral Constitution on the Church in the Modern World), this volume is relevant and far from cumbersome or heavy. Its style is thought-provoking and "poetic" enough to capture the interest of all, from the socialite to the bookworm rooted in his corner.

There is room for everyone in God's vast world and those who will marry have someone else created just for them, so to speak. They are destined to work out their earthly and eternal happiness together. How wonderful when young people realize this!

Success, however, never comes without hard work! The successful husband with a fine job and family did not arrive in those circumstances by accident. The happy mother whose children have all turned out well would hardly say: "Oh, it's nothing."

We've got to plot our course in life and follow that course. Who can risk "drifting" into a walk of life without a plan? Herein lies the worth of this book.

CONTENTS

Part One
ENGAGEMENT IS "FOR KEEPS"

13

Part Two
MARRIAGE—GOD'S OWN INVENTION

Part Three
CHOOSING ONE'S STATE IN LIFE

LOVE-THE REALITY OF IT

1

At some point a he and a her may come to the realization that there is something unique about their relationship. From this first feeling of love, what a long way they have to go! What "happened" without their fully realizing it at first will grow deeper as they come to know each other better—if they find that they are really meant for each other.

THINKING ALONG THE
MARRIAGE LINE

Young men and women mingling at a football game or on a crowded dance floor may easily scrutinize their contacts with the opposite sex. The girl might say: "Oh, he's just my type," or "He's not my type." The boy might say, "She's the kind I'd like for a wife some day," or "Poor guy who gets stuck with her!" It is natural to think in terms of a marriage partner because every human being seeks that "right one" who will understand him and love him alone. This desire is common to men and women alike, for God has designed the human heart that way. And someday that "right one" will be there, not fairy tale-like, but real.

Perhaps a look or a word will seal that meeting...while the pleasure of getting acquainted will daily grow more wonderful.

There can be meetings between a man and a woman where love is just a game and caprice ends in error and delusion.

There can be passionate meetings which devastate the heart and body, leaving a tormented soul, a dishonored name.

On the other hand, there are encounters in which two persons uplift one another and swear a loyalty which will remain untarnished for a lifetime. Possible? Yes, when men and women "choose" the company they keep.

A girl might ask herself before she starts getting serious about a boy:

Am I ready for this?

Am I modest, thoughtful, friendly?

Am I feminine, kind, mature?

Am I generous, or self-centered and vain?

Do I have common sense and principles?

Do I practice my faith?

If she fits the bill, then let her ask herself the following questions about the boy:

Is he ready for this?

Is he manly and decent or does he have a fairly bad reputation?

Is he dependable, punctual and mannerly?

Is he a good worker? Does he have a mature attitude
toward life?

Does he practice his faith?

The boy can ask the same questions about himself and
the girl. A lot of trouble, "false starts" and disappointments,
not to mention more serious things, can thus be avoided. And
when that "right one" comes along, this boy or girl has everything to give and nothing from the past to hide. Date only
marriage material!

Two young people are in love! Or *they think* they are in
love! But maybe it is just *romance,* which is a part of love or
can be an early stage of love. How does one tell the difference?

Love is the perfect union and agreement of one person
with another for the fulfillment of each other's perfection.

Romance, or plain passion, is the selfish encounter of
one life with another for base satisfaction.

Love seeks the good of the person loved; thus it is ready
to spend and sacrifice.

Passion seeks its own self-gratification.

Love is strong in times of difficulty; it holds true in times
of trial.

Romance can be just feverish selfishness, seeking the
person loved in order to satisfy its own desires. When contradicted, it may become irritated, angry, and then turn to
hate.

Love lights up a whole existence, blending two lives
into one.

Mere *romance* may flare for a few hours, a few days, a
few weeks. It is an encounter, but a brief one, often leaving
bitterness as its echo.

THEY CHOOSE EACH OTHER

At some point, a he and a her may come to the realization
that there is something unique about their relationship. From
this first feeling of love, what a long way they have to go! What
"happened" without their fully realizing it at first will grow
deeper as they come to know each other better—if they find

that they are really meant for each other. They will have to show each other sincerely what they are: their character, ideas, sentiments and tastes.

Every pretense and forced show will have to disappear and they will accept each other for what they are, each desiring to develop those individual qualities which unite them.

They will do their best to leave nothing vague between them, nothing that could cause disappointment or regret. With affectionate openness they will reveal and discuss their ideas and plans about themselves and others and above all, about the way they want their home to be—their human and religious ideals, their practical plans.

A GROWING LOVE

Love is always a fragile thing, especially in the beginning. And it can be deprived of many chances to develop if a couple give themselves without reserve to physical acts of affection. For this reason, they will control themselves carefully even when the wedding day is drawing near.

The wonders of a real love are not discovered in a day. Union of heart will be the joyful conquest of every day of their life together. Both will work at it, and each will find the greatest happiness not in looking out for himself or herself but in doing something for the other.

They won't be satisfied with a fundamental trust and fidelity; they will want to increase the beauty of their love by means of those acts of thoughtfulness and attention, in both the big things and the little ones, which make life together so delightful, which make painful things less painful, and which make it easier to forgive.

Their love will be so much a part of them that they will defend it at every turn. Knowing how distasteful they find it when off-color jokes about love and cynical remarks are aimed in their direction, they will never talk this way about their own relationship.

A growing love reaches into the regions of the soul and of prayer. When they go to the altar to pronounce their vows, it will certainly not be the first time—much less, the last— that love leads them to pray together. And God's blessing, His gift of special grace in the sacrament of Matrimony, will not be an isolated episode, hardly understood; it will be the crowning of a deep sentiment and a concept of life already common to both.

To the young women

Measuring Up "My Guy"...

A girl with definite standards will choose a husband carefully. Keeping the steady barometer of "reality" in front of her she will remember the character qualities which really measure a person's worth. The fellow who is the popularity winner, who is eligible, handsome and generally "Mr. Big" is the one she may think she secretly loves (just as all the other girls do). But besides the fact that he isn't even aware of her existence, he may also be as conceited and self-centered as can be. Now, Joe, on the other hand, is a nice average boy. His buddies like him a lot. He's not handsome, but nice looking in an average sort of way, and has many wonderful qualities which become more and more apparent as she gets to know him. He's no match for "Mr. Big" in a

popularity poll, but when it comes to that *life-time credit rating*, Joe's victory is an easy one.

Experience teaches that the campus noise-makers of yesterday are too often the stragglers in life today, whereas the boys who studied hard and plodded along went on to become "greats." They were thinkers instead of talkers. They were learning instead of giving all the answers.

Don't look for your partner *front and center*. Look around. Observe.... After all, once married, a happy "living together" is no accident. It is bought with the constant practice of self-denial, kindness, patience, understanding and mutual co-operation. The person thinking about marriage should ponder on this.

WITH WHOM CAN I BUILD A LIFE?

What if romance with that certain "he" involves some big obstacles? Such as...

...a partner inclined to drink

Heavy drinking may be the dangerous prelude to unhappiness and evil. A great deal of suffering and misery is connected with alcoholism for all concerned.

If you notice that the boy you love needs a drink to be happy and is often with the "guys" at the local bar, go slow and think things over. These habits are easily put aside at the church altar but just might grow with the passing of time....

...that divorced man

A young woman, even if she considers herself mature enough to know her own mind, should never date a divorced man of any faith, because she runs the risk of becoming involved in an invalid marriage. The world is so big.... Let a girl choose from the immense harvest of "eligibles." By dating one whom she cannot rightfully marry, she may spoil her chances of meeting that *someone* with whom she could be blessed with a happy marriage.

Even if the Catholic party's previous marriage was performed by a Justice of the Peace or minister, and therefore was invalid, and even though his first marital failure was undoubtedly not his own doing, the bitter memories and the sting remain. A hasty second marriage is no solution to his problem. The wise girl does not flatter herself that she is the perfect woman who will wash away all his past hurts. Let her fall back on *reality*, and at least ask herself the question: what if his second marriage follows the same course the first one took?

...jealousy—phantom torture

What should a girl do if her fiance constantly tortures himself and her with his suspicions and questions about her dates previous to their engagement? Will his jealousy result in an unhappy marriage?

First of all, she must let him know that it was perfectly right for her to have gone out with other young men before becoming engaged. Jealousy over a fiance's former dates is unfair and unrealistic. As a matter of fact, of all the others she dated, she chose him. This is a compliment, after all!

Some men are inclined to be mistrustful and can manage to find evil where there just isn't any. If this is the case, no matter how faithful his partner is to him, the jealous man will probably never be satisfied or let his partner live a normal, happy life.

As a husband, the jealous man can become a source of immeasurable misery both to himself and his wife. If there is no sign of a change, a girl had better break off a relationship that can only mean real suffering to her in married life. If she were already married, there would be nothing to say but: "Patiently carry the cross you have chosen for yourself! Do your duty and trust in God, who alone can make every burden light." However, for one who is engaged, there is still time, precious time, to think twice.

HAVE I GOT WHAT IT TAKES?...

"Who shall find a valiant woman?
Far and from the uttermost coasts is the price of her.
The heart of her husband trusts her."

Proverbs 31:10

Frederick Ozanam wrote this prayer for an ideal wife:
"Grant, O Lord,
that the woman I marry
may possess that exterior loveliness
and charm which keep a man
from feeling dissatisfied,
but most of all, I beg You

that she may possess
a beautiful soul,
adorned with great virtue,
that she may be better than I,
that she may draw me
toward the higher things,
and not drag me down.
I ask You to make her generous,
for I am weak;
fervent, for I am lukewarm in the things of God;
and finally, compassionate,
that I may not have to feel humiliated at
my inferiority to her."

A woman very readily exerts influence on the moral character of her fiance. If she is good, she inspires him for the good. If she has cheapened herself, she degrades him. She kills the most endearing qualities of the man, lessening his abilities, and sapping his spirit, leaving him broken and old before his time.

The man who finds a good girl feels better for loving her. Besides the excitement of love, he feels even in his quieter moments that he is doing the right thing, the best thing.

The engaged girl who knows how to keep her love pure and chaste will command her fiance's respect and make him consider himself really lucky to be getting her. Her strength of character will convince him that she has what it takes to be faithful when things get rough.

The more the affection of an engaged couple is chaste and serious, the more enduring and joyous is their love as husband and wife.

To the young men

What Kind of Girl Do I Really Want?

How to pick a wife—now that's no easy task. Past experience means much in any prudent human judgment. We are so inclined to learn by *trial and error;* in fact, we are all familiar with such sayings as *older and wiser.* But in the choice of a wife everything is different.

Past experience? There isn't any.

Trial and error? No second chances are allowed. One marriage, one wife for a lifetime.

Older and wiser? This again rarely applies. Most people getting married are young and, even with the best of good will, readily admit they have a lot to learn.

What shall they do, then? Take a chance? This doesn't make sense, does it? A life based on chance is a foolish man's game.

One thing a fellow can do then. He can listen to the good advice of parents and priests and read reliable books on marriage. These will furnish the material for forming his own standards. Setting rules for himself and rules that he expects a girl to measure up to will be a fine start.

She is blond and beautiful, coy and clever, a real "Miss Personality." Who couldn't help but notice her? She is usually the topic of conversation. To win her heart would make any man happy. She probably is a fine girl and yet...looks aren't everything.

Now, take an honest glance at your mother. From an objective point of view, *is she beautiful?* More than likely not. And yet every boy thinks his mother is beautiful because of her goodness, her self-sacrifice, her dedication, her wonderful laugh, her warm personality. Maybe her face has gathered a few wrinkles over the years; her hands are a bit gnarled and red, and those size nine dresses are just a vague memory, but her beauty hasn't faded because hers isn't just physical attractiveness; it is a beauty of soul and character. That is why, after so many years, her husband still feels a hidden joy when he comes home from work at night and finds her waiting there.

Look for a girl of goodness and quality. Hers is a beauty which will never disappear.

WHERE TO FIND HER

After graduation from high school or college, or a return from the service, it is sometimes hard to meet new friends. The best advice is to "hang around" with the people and in the places where the right kind of girl is apt to be.

From among girls with a good reputation, about whose purity and self-respect nobody can say anything, a boy can look for one who especially appeals to him. He won't find himself powerfully attracted to someone whom he can't respect now and can't picture as the mother of his children.

A good place to meet someone who would make a partner of whom one could be proud is at parish or community centers where a lot of good things are going on and a lot of energy and heart is being given for the benefit of others.

PARTNER MATERIAL

Not everything in a skirt is desirable "partner material." A defective character in a girl is not always as quickly spotted as in a boy. However, there are some cues to watch for, and some types to be avoided, if a boy wants to assure himself of a happy married life.

When a girl consistently begins every conversation and every sentence with the big "I," beware. That "I" is deeper than "skin deep" and may cause real trouble later on. All one needs do is contradict the all-important "I" and a small-scale revolution breaks out. If a girl is not mature enough to have some thought of others, she is not mature enough for marriage.

A sense of humor is indispensable in a marriage partner, but giddiness and lightheadedness are out of place. A boy should think twice before considering as a life partner a girl who does not have self-control. She knows only how to joke, even when the situation is anything but a joking matter. Everything is hilariously funny, and everyone knows it by her loud, shrill laughter. She tries to be happy-go-lucky but ends up making a fool of herself and her date. This type of girl will find difficulty in taking marriage seriously. She will laugh off responsibilities and become bored when serious problems must be discussed. The greater burden of the marriage will fall on her unfortunate partner, and he will have to work out the difficulties alone.

Constructive criticism builds, whereas destructive criticism destroys everything in its path. The girl who continually finds fault with everyone and everything is doing more damage than a bulldozer! In a few sharp words she can tear down a reputation it took someone seventeen or more years to build. No one is exempt from her cryptic remarks, not even the one she thinks she loves. A marriage partner with this defect can bring a marriage to a quick and bitter end.

A fellow looking for a marriage partner almost automatically shys away from the girl who has "been around too much." The coy flirt is not as attractive as she thinks she appears. Her flirtatious ways are no longer so cute when she has "Mrs." before her name. The full trust that her husband should place in her is tarnished by doubts and uncertainties. Maybe she only flirts...but can he be sure? A marriage cannot be built on doubts. Each partner must be able to trust the other explicitly, in all circumstances and at all times. Flirting and matrimony don't mix!

ON THE DOLLAR SIDE

In order to marry, a man's salary should be large enough to pay the rent of a decent apartment and the expenses of food and clothing. There should even be something left over to put in the bank for future needs. It must be sufficient, above all, to support a family, for besides being a loving companionship, marriage means especially *parenthood.*

For these reasons, a boy still in college, for example, is scarcely in a good position to marry. He should wait until he finishes his education and secures a steady job.

Because of the demands of his fiancée, a young man may realize that his salary will have to be more than just sufficient. However, a woman who truly loves a man will not expect him to provide an expensive apartment, costly furniture and other luxuries over and above their level of income. If he finds he is expected to do so, he would be wiser to look for someone less exacting and more understanding, one who does not judge a man's worth by his bank book. For he must keep in mind that a girl who is so demanding before marriage will most likely not be a good wife and manager of a home.

AGE DIFFERENCES

How many years difference should there be between marriage partners?

Fifteen years? This is too great a difference, because when the wife is forty-five years old, for instance, her husband will be sixty. There will be too great a difference in their tastes, ideas and physical tendencies. This might cause their love for one another to grow cold or to cease altogether.

Ten years? This difference still seems to be too great for the same reason.

Six, five, four years? These seem to be the more acceptable age differences.

Generally, it is the man who should be older than the woman, because he must be able to support a family before he can prudently marry.

However, age difference in itself is not an important factor in marital happiness. "Age is a relative factor," says Father J. L. Thomas, S.J. "It is not how old you are, but *what you are* that makes for success in marriage."

DOLLAR FOR DOLLAR?

The education and vocational instruction of their children is the parents' duty. Therefore they cannot require their children to put off marriage until they have been repaid dollar for dollar the expenses incurred in giving them a proper education for a position in life.

However, if the parents are in need, it is the children's duty, naturally, to take care of their parents, who gave them life and sacrificed themselves for their welfare.

"A fairly early marriage," says Cardinal Mindszenty, "is not only beneficial for the morals of the young couple, but also carries with it advantages for the children they hope to have. For when the parents are young at the time of marriage, they have, humanly speaking, a greater assurance of living to rear their children than they would have if they married late in life. Besides, in an early marriage the expectancy of children is greater than in marriage contracted later in life."

Tale of the "Ifs" and the "Whoms"

Parents, as wonderful as they may be, do not have the right to decide *if* and *whom* their children should marry. One may exercise the natural right to live singly if he or she so desires; moreover, the state of virginity or celibacy, embraced for the love of God, is higher even than the married state.

Although it is a person's God-given right to marry whomever he wishes, you can't lose by talking it over with your parents before definitely deciding to marry.

Should parental advice be followed? There may be some special situation where it need not, yet generally one who listens to his parents is the happiest in marriage, whereas he who does not often has much cause to deeply regret that he didn't. After all, who more than they have at heart the best interests of their young people? The advice of mom and dad is packed with worth, for they are graduates of that age-old *School of Experience.* It is only right, therefore, that their children turn to them for advice in so important a matter as the choice of a life partner. And good parents, on the other hand, advise prudently, while leaving their sons and daughters a certain freedom in choosing.

This is ordinarily the way things are, yet perhaps we should glance at a few possible exceptions. Sad to say, there are parents, for instance, who oppose a son's or daughter's choice solely because of nationality differences.

Now, nationality differences do exist, and in matters of the home there are different customs regarding food, the role and influence of relatives, the bringing up of children, etc.

However, do differences in nationality really create difficulties in marriage?

Well, they become important only if they mean that husband and wife will have radically different views on such essential points as how a family functions, and the status and roles of husband, wife and children.

If the man and woman who intend to marry do share the same ideas regarding the above matters, that is what counts. Nationality differences, in themselves, do not.

To the great *melting pot* which is America all the nations of the world have lent the best ingredients from their cultures. The United States has no one culture to claim for its own. Great men and women representing every land on earth came and brought with them their marvelous and varied customs, manners and fine qualities of character. If America can be a blend of all cultures, then each individual can most certainly accept the various cultures and incorporate them into his own way of life.

A young man, for instance, who knows that the girl of his choice shares his views regarding the nature and purpose of marriage and family relationships, and who finds his parents strenuously objecting only because of her nationality, should try to change their view. Failing in that, he may have to respectfully ignore their attitude.

There also may be parents who never seem to be satisfied with the choices their sons or daughters make. They find fault with every boy their precious daughter brings home. That one is too short.... Another, too quiet.... Still another holds no promise for the future. And so the list goes on. No one is good enough for their girl!

If a girl realizes, after carefully considering her parents' advice, that this is true in her case, she should make her own decision. No man is perfect, as she herself is not perfect. A mature girl should be able to decide for herself whether or not her boyfriend has the qualities to be looked for in a marriage partner. She must judge the situation honestly, practically,...not letting her emotions take over. The same holds for the young man who is choosing a wife. *For all my life* the bride and groom say on their wedding day. Let those words ring in the ears of young men and women choosing their life's partner: *For all my life!*

A fundamental and essential ingredient of a happy marriage is a good supply of plain, ordinary *common sense* in both parties. But getting down to specifics, in regard to the man she intends to marry, *a girl should ask herself:*

Does he value religion?

Is he a person who knows how to take responsibility, who can keep a job and is capable of supporting a family?

Does he act his age, exercise self-control, show emotional maturity?

Does he show respect for me and does he share my sense of values?

Is he thoughtful and considerate, willing to give in often or, at least, to compromise?

Is he polite and courteous with my parents and other members of my family?

Is he confident and manly when confronted with a tough situation?

In regard to the girl, the boy should ask himself:

Does she value religion?

Is she appreciative and thoughtful? Does she come to the assistance of others with generosity and tact?

How does she act at home? Is she good at cooking and housekeeping?

Does home life mean a lot to her?

Is she considerate and affectionate toward her parents?

Is she honest and straightforward with everyone?

Is she neat and attractive without going to extremes in attempting to be glamorous?

Is she an attentive and sympathetic listener?

When a young woman (or man) can sincerely answer "yes" to these questions, she (or he) may seriously consider marriage even if parents feel otherwise.

It should also be remembered that the fullest measure of marital happiness will be found with a partner with whom one shares similar convictions and interests.

In conclusion, there may be times when parental advice can be prudently ignored. In these cases, young men and women do very well to seek the advice of others they trust— their pastor or confessor, first of all. By so doing, they may feel more certain of the wisdom of their choice. However, as we stressed in the beginning, the times when such parental advice may be ignored are rare exceptions.

On the other hand, it has proved true time and again that a lot of people would have been spared their present heartaches if they had listened....

To Each His Own

At the risk of sounding *un-ecumenical* we bring up a topic which has always been rather a sensitive point. We ask plainly: *What about marriages between Catholics and non-Catholics?*

The Vatican's *Instruction on Mixed Marriage* states:

"Let all the Shepherds teach the faithful the religious importance and value of this sacrament (of Matrimony). Let them gravely warn the faithful of the difficulties and dangers which are inherent in contracting a marriage with a Christian non-Catholic, and much more with a non-Christian. By all suitable means let them bring it about that young people contract marriage with a Catholic party."

Notice in the above paragraph the phrase, *let them gravely warn the faithful of the difficulties and dangers....* Does this sound rather severe in our liberal age? Not really, when we recall that the Church speaks with twenty centuries of experience behind it. History is a great teacher.

The reality of the difficulties connected with mixed marriages is proven by the fact that not only Catholic but also

Protestant and Jewish leaders constantly urge their flocks to marry those of their own faith.

What are some of these difficulties?

In a mixed marriage there may often be conflicting views on vital matters, and constant disagreement can wear down even the strongest affection. Arguments can easily arise over issues of birth control and the Catholic education of the children, for instance. Worse yet, despite promises, the non-Catholic may begin to make it very hard for his or her partner to practice the faith and to have the children baptized Catholic.

Even if none of these difficulties turn up, religion is such a vital force in one's life that when a couple cannot share it, they feel something missing in their union. Each tries alone to grow in his own faith without offending the other. A "we-don't-discuss-it-policy" often seems the only solution, but again, here we have two people joined in the closest relationship who don't talk together about the things that mean the most.

Unfortunately, one or the other often begins to stop practicing his faith. Moreover, it is a statistical fact that many children of mixed marriages are lost to the Church.

For all these reasons, a truthful discussion of mixed marriages must indicate the dangers and difficulties involved.

It must also be pointed out, however, that mixed marriages can be opportunities for grace, for the entrance of the non-Catholic into the church. And these marriages are sacramental.

Moreover, if after weighing the problems involved and their own strength of faith, after agreeing on the obligations of married life, a couple enters into a mixed marriage, they should plan from the start to work together in the area of religion — with great trust in God!

CHURCH LAW AND MIXED MARRIAGES

When the Church permits a mixed marriage, it generally requires that only a Catholic ceremony be used. Also for a Catholic to be married validly, whether his partner is Catholic or non-Catholic, the presence of an authorized priest and two witnesses is required except in certain special instances as mentioned further on.

"Peculiar conditions of our age," states the Vatican's *Instruction on Mixed Marriage,* "which in a short time have brought such important changes into the social and family life, have made the observance of the canonical discipline in regard to mixed marriages more difficult than in times past.

"Under these circumstances it now happens that communications, acquaintances, and contacts of Catholics and non-Catholics are more frequent, and so the bonds of friendship are more easily established between them which, as is evident from experience, are wont to bring on more frequent occasions of mixed marriages."

The Church, practical as ever, realizing that the problem is with us and is growing, has, through the mouth of her Vicar, Pope Paul VI, issued directives which the above-mentioned *Instruction* says "if verified by experience will be inserted in a fixed and definitive way in the Code of Canon Law which is now being revised."

The following rules are quoted from the *Instruction on Mixed Marriage:*

1. It should always be kept in mind that danger to the faith is to be warded off from the Catholic spouse and that the education of the child in the Catholic religion must be cared for diligently.

2. The local Ordinary (the bishop) or the pastor of the Catholic party will take care to inculcate in grave words the obligation of always providing for the baptism and education of the future offspring in the Catholic religion. The fulfillment of this obligation will be assured by the explicit promise or guarantee made by the same Catholic party.

3. The non-Catholic party with due respect, but in a clear manner, is certainly to be informed of the Catholic teaching about the dignity of matrimony and especially about its chief qualities which are *unity* and *indissolubility.*
The grave obligation of the Catholic spouse to guard, preserve, profess his (her) own faith and to baptize and educate in that faith the offspring that may be born must be made known to the same non-Catholic party.

Since this obligation must be safeguarded, the non-Catholic party entering marriage is to be invited to promise sincerely and openly that he will in no way impede this obligation. If, however, the non-Catholic party thinks that he cannot make this promise without violating his own conscience the Ordinary is to refer the case with all its circumstances to the Holy See.

4. Although by the ordinary law these promises are to be given in writing, it is, however, in the power of the Ordinary to decide, either in general or in individual cases, whether this promise of the Catholic party or the non-Catholic party or of both is to be given in writing or not, and likewise to determine how this is to be entered in the marriage records.

The local bishop may permit in the celebration of mixed marriages the use of sacred rites, the customary blessing and the sermon.

"Any celebration of a marriage," adds the *Instruction on Mixed Marriage*, "before a Catholic priest and a non-Catholic minister in which each one simultaneously carries out his own rite must be avoided absolutely. Nevertheless, there is no objection that the non-Catholic minister speak some words of congratulation and exhortation after the religious ceremony is concluded, and that some prayers be recited with the non-Catholics. All this may be done with the approval of the local Ordinary and the use of timely precautions to avoid danger of astonishment."

"Brethren of other Churches," states the *Directory on Ecumenism*, "may act as bridesmaid or best man at a wedding in a Catholic church. A Catholic, too, can be best man or bridesmaid at a marriage properly celebrated among separated brethren."

At times, for special reasons, the Church makes exceptions to its regulations on the celebration of marriage. Any Catholic who desires further information on these matters may always obtain it from his parish priest.

CATHOLIC - ORTHODOX CONCESSION

The increasing frequency of mixed marriages between Oriental Catholics and non-Catholic Oriental Christians in the eastern patriarchates and eparchies as well as in the Latin dioceses themselves, and the necessity of coping with the inconveniences resulting from this, were the reasons why the Second Vatican Ecumenical Council decreed: "When Oriental Catholics enter into marriage with baptized non-Catholic Orientals the canonical form for the celebration of such marriages obliges only for lawfulness; for their validity, the presence of a sacred minister suffices, as long as the other requirements of the law are observed" (Decr. on Catholic Churches of Eastern Rite, 18).

CONCESSION TO INCLUDE LATIN CHURCHES

In the exceptional circumstances of today, mixed marriages between the Catholic faithful of the Latin rite and non-Catholic Oriental faithful are taking place and the variety in canonical disciplines has brought about many grave difficulties both in the East and the West. For this reason petitions from various regions have been addressed to the Supreme Pontiff asking that he be pleased to unify canonical discipline in this matter by also permitting to Catholics of the Latin rite what has been decreed for Catholics of the Eastern rite.

His Holiness, our Pope, Paul VI, by divine providence, after mature reflection and diligent investigation, has resolved to agree to the petitions and desires addressed to him and, as a means of preventing invalid marriages between the faithful of the Latin rite and the non-Catholic Christian faithful of the Oriental rites, of showing proper regard for the permanence and sanctity of marriages, and of promoting charity between the Catholic faithful and the non-Catholic Oriental faithful, he has kindly granted that, when Catholics, whether they be Orientals or Latins contract marriage with non-Catholic Oriental faithful, the canonical form for the celebration of these marriages obliges only for lawfulness; for validity the presence of a sacred minister suffices, as long as the other requirements of the law are observed (Decr. on Mixed Marriages between Catholics and Baptized, Non-Catholic Orientals).

All care should be taken that, under the guidance of the pastors, such marriages be carefully entered into the prescribed registers as soon as possible; this prescription also holds when Catholic Orientals enter marriage with baptized non-Catholic Orientals according to the norm of the conciliar decree on the Catholic Oriental Churches, n. 18.

In conformity with the holiness of marriage itself, non-Catholic ministers are reverently and earnestly requested to cooperate in the task of registering marriages in the books of the Catholic party, whether of the Latin or Oriental rite.

Ordinaries of the place, who grant the dispensation from the impediment of mixed religion, are likewise given the faculty of dispensing from the obligation of observing canonical form for lawfulness if there exist difficulties which, according to their prudent judgment, require this dispensation (Decr. on Mixed Marriages between Catholics and Baptized, Non-Catholic Orientals).

A TIME FOR TESTING

2

Engagement is a time of testing to see if a couple will make suitable partners for life. It is a time of preparation for the day when they will utter a solemn promise—that day when they will unite for life.

Her face is radiant as she steps through the front door, pulling her boyfriend by the hand. She calls, "Mom, Dad, come on in the living room for a minute."

From one direction comes Mom with a pot holder and salt shaker; from another comes Dad. "Well, what is all this?" they both exclaim. "Look," their daughter sings, stretching out her left hand which has just been enhanced with a dazzling diamond ring. "Tom and I are engaged."

Mom gulps a bit and her eyes grow shiny. Dad stares... speechless for just a second, and then mumbles quiet "congratulations." They glance at each other, sharing the realization that their daughter has grown up. She is on the threshold of a new life....

Engagement is a time of *testing* to see if a couple will make suitable partners for life. It is for those who are old enough and are ready to shoulder the responsibilities of married life. Couples should keep in mind that the engagement is a *time of preparation* for the day when they will utter a solemn promise—that day when they will unite themselves for life, "for better, for worse, for richer, for poorer...."

Once these words are spoken, there is no turning back.

Engagement is a *mutual promise of marriage.* Regarding its duration the Church has no explicit rule, but normally from six months to a year should suffice. Young couples in love make it a time of mutual self-revelation, of joyful discovery, of growth in trust and friendship. Yes, friendship, too, because lovers are not just lovers. They are friends. Then it grows easy to talk naturally and simply about important topics like finances, health, social relations, etc., to prevent future quarrels.

Engagement is a time of *observation.* Each person can view his or her partner in real situations, when they are alone, when walking down a street, on a Sunday afternoon drive, with each other's family, at church on Sunday, at a party, at a dance, with his or her friends, etc. Slowly, their characters unfold to each other's view, becoming crystal clear, and their love grows more firm, more mature.

40

3.

Should an engaged couple eventually realize that they are not meant for each other and that their marriage would be a mistake, they should face the fact with honesty and break the engagement at once. What could be more tragic than to have to spend one's entire life with a partner who is cold and distant?

Marriage means nothing less than the intimate union of two hearts living out their lives together. This is *marriage* as Christ intended it, blessed at Cana and crowned with the dignity of a *sacrament*. Thus it is that marriage leads to heaven.

PRE-CANA CONFERENCES

Across the United States engaged couples are offered the opportunity to attend Pre-Cana conferences run by the diocese to which they belong. Timely, up-to-date and very important, the talks develop the themes of friendship, love, togetherness in marriage and Christ as the principal partner.

A priest, a physician and married couples usually make up the team giving the conferences.

The priest imparts ideas concerning the theology of marriage. The physician penetrates the concepts dealing with the physical and psychological relationship of each partner to the other. The husband and wife team give many practical pointers, sharing the benefit of many of their own experiences.

Discussion topics — dialogue — stimulate discussions ranging from working wives to arguments. Then, the engagement rings are blessed.

These conferences take so little time and reap such good results.

LONG ENGAGEMENTS

While hasty marriages reveal tragic results, long engagements bring their problems, too.

Therefore, as soon as the promise to marry is made, a definite date for the wedding should be set. Unless there are unavoidable difficulties, the engagement should not be prolonged, for the couple may become a source of dangerous temptation to each other.

Moreover, during a long engagement someone else may enter on the scene and if the engagement is broken, it may be very hard for the one left alone to find a new love after being "out of circulation" for so long.

WHERE SHALL WE GO TONIGHT?

The best place for engaged couples to pass their hours together is at home with the family—hers or his. Yes, a boy can best discover his future wife's real character while viewing her with the members of her family. By observing how she treats her mother, her father, her brothers and sisters, he will know what to expect when they are married, for she will treat him the same way. The way she cleans (or doesn't clean), cooks (or doesn't cook) in her own home now will let him know what to expect in their home of the future.

Marriage is a wonderful thing, but it has never been known to work miracles. Hence, it is essential to discover beforehand the character and virtues of a future partner. This cannot be done, however, if he or she is seen only on the ball-room floor, at the beach, or in the movie theater!

The boy should bring his girl home to visit his family, too. There she can observe how he treats and respects his mother, and she will have a good idea of how he will treat her.

Furthermore, a couple should try to do many things together, especially to attend Sunday Mass.

Whenever possible, it is always good to "double date" because moral security is greater and it's fun to share the company of other engaged couples.

A KISS—BOND OR BETRAYAL

The late Father Daniel A. Lord, S.J., in his book, *Questions I'm Asked about Marriage*, once wrote:

"A kiss between a man and a woman is a symbol. It is the sign of a deep affection; it is the expression of the man's and the woman's desire to bind that affection in marriage. It is an external manifestation of love.

"...The careless giving and receiving of kisses between a man and a woman should rarely be tolerated. To allow to a chance or a casual companion of an evening the same symbolic expression by which a man and a woman pledge undying love is to do something quite out of line. There is in addition the well-known fact that a kiss may be the occasion of passion. A kiss begun in friendship can easily end in passion, in which case a kiss becomes matter for serious consideration."

A kiss may light the fires of passion. Then it becomes a *traitor's kiss*, in a sense, for it is given not to show affection and love but to seek satisfaction, to pluck from the receiver not her pledge of fidelity, but her human capabilities of satiating the giver's sensual desires. A foolish kiss seems to promise happiness, but is only a *mirage*. The kiss which leads to unlawful intimacies breaks and divides. It never seals a love.

Problems regarding passionate kissing are best solved in the confessional, where they should be stated simply and modestly.

"The high-type girl," continues Father Lord, "will save her kisses for the day when she will give them to the man she really loves and to the children she will bear. And before she kisses a man, she will certainly consider the fact that she may be placing him in the danger of sinful passion.

"The high-type young man will ask of the girl nothing that will cheapen her or the sacred symbols by which she manifests her love. And certainly he will be most unwilling to endanger her innocence, much less to excite her passions to the point of sin."

Couples who are truly in love know that nothing is more intense and more beautiful than real love which is much more than the fever of the senses. Sound incredible in our day and age? *It is not. It is reality.*

Sensual love dies when the desire is satisfied. Holy Scripture provides an unforgettable example of this fickleness of sensual love in the story of Amnon and Thamar. Amnon, a son of David, "fell sick for the love of" Thamar, his half-sister. Working out a clever scheme, he managed to be left alone with the beautiful girl and then, taking advantage of his superior strength, he satisfied his impure desires, despite her pleas and protests.

No sooner had Amnon succeeded in his intent than he roughly dismissed Thamar: "Then Amnon hated her with an exceeding great hatred: so that the hatred with which he hated her was greater than the love with which he had loved her before. And Amnon said to her, 'Arise and get out of here.' She answered him, 'This evil which now you do against me, in driving me away, is greater than that which you did before.' And he would not listen to her. But calling the servants who ministered to him, he said, 'Thrust this woman out from me, and shut the door after her' " (2 Kings).

HOW IS LOVE MEASURED?

The greatest mistake two engaged people can make is to believe that their love is to be measured by the intensity of their sensual attraction....

True and lasting love is to be found in the will, not in the emotions. It is the contact of one soul with another for their common perfection. "If love does not climb," says Bishop Sheen, "it falls. If, like the flame, love does not burn upward to the sun, it burns downward to destroy. If sex does not mount to heaven, it descends into hell."

God has put into human beings certain instincts and powers. In fact, if man and woman were not strongly attracted to each other, there would be no marriage, and the human race would perish. These powers, however, are to be used only in the state of matrimony.

Holy Scripture says: "And God created man to his own image; to the image of God he created him. Male and female he created them. And God blessed them saying: Increase and multiply, and fill the earth" (Gen. 1:27-28).

To use merely for one's own pleasure and gratification the instincts and powers given by God for the purpose of instituting the family and continuing the human race would be a grave evil against nature and against the will of God.

Moreover, the observance of conjugal fidelity will prove difficult for those who, before marriage, do not resist the temptations of the flesh.

Impurity, in fact, is poison for the family and for society and if it becomes a national vice, it spells the fall of states and peoples.

When a young man shows a desire to take certain liberties, such as necking and petting, that is, impure touches and embraces that excite the passions, his fiancée should refuse with modesty and firmness. Thus she will win the admiration and respect of the man she loves and not his scorn for her looseness....

RECIPE FOR MARRIAGE:
SEX? LOVE? GRACE?

A group of busy wives and mothers met for their Tuesday evening discussion club. The priest-moderator led the middle-aged women on to the topic of marriage. All, he knew, were happily married, with children near grown, and so they would certainly feel qualified to speak about such a topic.

"What, in your opinion," he asked the group, "is the first ingredient for a happy marriage?

The women were quiet for a moment. Then the answers came, spontaneous and sincere. "Certainly not sex," one woman responded. The others quickly agreed.

"I think the primary ingredient would be *love*," another answered. The majority thought the same.

If one were to give some advice to a young couple planning to get married, he might say something like this:
Reflect...and make sure that your love is sincere and
deep; a love which wants to give and not just take;
a personal, exclusive love with no secret desires
for someone else.
Only such a love can carry you over the inevitable
troubles and obstacles which come to every couple,
and last in one form or another for a lifetime.
Soon you will both bear the same name! Soon you
will realize the happiness of which you have dreamed —
provided, however, that now you have freely chosen
one another, that your love is spontaneous and that
you have decided to marry because you love each other.
Do not marry if you do not love, because a marriage
without love leads to love outside of marriage.
Love! Love your future partner and even all your in-laws.
Love one another strongly and constantly, in spite of
the defects which you will discover as time goes by....
And you will experience genuine marital happiness.

AND WHAT ABOUT GRACE?

From what we have just said, then, it seems that the women were right — love is the answer. Or is it? Marriage is a community of love, a covenant, a commitment, a promise which involves the whole person for life. It is a great sacrament, a sign, a bond. It has its special role in the total plan of salvation.

"Matrimony according to the will of God continues the work of the first creation (Gen. 2:18); and considered within the total plan of salvation, it even acquires a new meaning and a new value. Jesus, in fact, has restored its original dignity (Mt. 19:3-8), has honored it (John 2:1-11), and has raised it to the dignity of a sacrament and of a mysterious symbol of His own union with the Church (Eph. 5:32).

"Thus, Christian couples walk together toward their heavenly fatherland in the exercise of mutual love, in the fulfillment of their particular obligations, and in striving for the sanctity proper to them" (Encycl. "Priestly Celibacy").

Now, if marriage is all this, knowing our weak human nature, doesn't it stand to reason that *God's grace* is the most essential factor in any marriage?

Being a sacrament as Baptism or Confirmation, etc., Matrimony increases sanctifying grace in the soul and entitles those who receive it to special graces to help them fulfill the duties of the married state.

To be aware of these graces to which married people have a claim is to be aware of a storehouse of strength and encouragement for those days "Mother told me would come." For every difficulty, obligation and responsibility in married life, God gives a special grace so that these duties may be fulfilled with love and Christian joy.

By means of the reciprocal personal gift of self, proper and exclusive to them, husband and wife tend towards the communion of their beings in view of mutual personal perfection, to collaborate with God in the generation and education of new lives. The attainment of this end is not always smooth riding. The coming of a new child can mean heroic sacrifice in some cases. In every case it requires a certain amount of self-sacrifice. But where the grace of God is present, where the grace of the sacrament is accepted, difficulties become easier and love makes one blind to hardships.

Following is part of a letter from a young woman who seems to have forgotten that a child means sacrifice.

"You can't imagine our joy at being parents! For us it is the most beautiful thing in this world — to be happy, preoccupied, all intent on the little creature that is ours. These are the things that give true meaning to married life. How grateful we are to God for such a tremendous gift. In the first place our baby is demanding love, not indifference. The baby is a reminder that, after God, our whole life must be centered on our growing family who will fill our life with many joys and consolations."

LOVE? ... LOVE? ... LOVE? ...

It carries a variety of meanings—that word "love." Some think of it simply in terms of love of neighbor. Well, any love of neighbor, even if it be the love for the man or woman one plans to spend a lifetime with, must be rooted in God. It was St. John the Apostle who wrote: "God is love, and he who abides in love abides in God, and God in him." Love of God gives to married couples the help, the grace, the strength they need to live their "vocation of love."

Without God's grace, even the most strong-willed man or woman will find himself or herself floundering and falling. Left to ourselves life would be a frightful failure. Grace makes two ordinary people capable of obligations of their state in life, makes them able and loving partners and parents, makes them responsible and self-sacrificing. Grace—not ourselves! That is the secret of every successful life. The saints became saints with the help of God's grace. There is no other way.

Grace comes through prayer and the sacraments. Family prayer is ever powerful: "Where two or more are gathered together in my name there am I in the midst of them." This is *love*, the meaning behind the word, a love which grows with grace.

The sacramental grace of matrimony is a real thing. It is there when it is needed. It makes itself felt, strengthens love, fosters understanding of the other's views, ways and opinions. Sacramental grace steps in when patience wears thin, when one feels like contradicting, arguing, answering with a sharp remark. It makes living together a learning experience, a school of love and virtue. It makes striving for perfection, for union with God possible. The sacramental grace of matrimony works in those small everyday situations that constitute life.

Without grace matrimony becomes unbearable, and one miserable day follows another until the couple "can't take it any more" and give up. This is not living. This is not fulfilling all the marvelous capacities God has placed in us.

No doubt most young people are aware of the natural effects of matrimony. *The supernatural effects are just as real.* A lopsided view of marriage is a danger in a world where materialism holds the foreground. A balanced view of marriage leads to a realistic outlook and a one hundred per cent better chance for marriage where each one loves the other and both love God, the only Font of lasting happiness.

PASSIONS, EMOTIONS AN

3

Mature love spots the essential goodness in a person and does not lose sight of this quality even when human failings and faults make themselves evident.

Everyone has heard of whirlwind engagements. If we followed one through the years of married life, we might be surprised at an outcome so opposite to that passionate first love.

A young man and woman, sure of their love for one another, could not bear the thought of waiting. Two short weeks of acquaintance and then the marriage vows! What were his interests, his ideas on vital issues, on the essential purpose of married life, his character, etc.? She didn't know. She only knew that she loved him.... What kind of a wife would she make? Did she possess qualities one looks for in a good mother, was she willing to sacrifice and give in? He didn't know...but he loved her! This "love" did not last long. Soon the fights began, the unending annoyances, nagging and picking. Personality clashes and incompatibility were the normal fare of the day.

Their family grew to ten children, which under happier circumstances might have led to a joyful, small community of love. However, with each new child the mother pitied herself a little more. The father was a stranger to unselfish love and self-sacrifice. They were both so continually occupied with themselves that the children grew up on their own, with neither the good example nor the guidance of their parents. More than one spent time in a house of correction. When the couple reached their forties, still without even a basic understanding of one another, they obtained a legal divorce and went their separate ways alone.

Unfortunately, this is a true story. But they were in love.... Or were they?... Emotions and feelings play a far greater role in our lives than most people care to admit. Emotions, or passions, are powers placed in us by God. When controlled and well channelled, they become motivators helping toward the attainment of a goal. They give spice to life and dynamism in living. Can anyone imagine even one day spent without encountering either our own emotions or those of others? Life would be pretty gray!

Some young people, however, have not matured to the point of being able to distinguish between a feeling or emotion, and the real thing. What a mature person would call *infatuation*, they call love.

As we can all testify, emotions or feelings are extremely changeable. One day we are up, the next day we are down. One day the whole world is our friend, the next day we feel like the whole world is against us! *Most people do not have to be convinced that emotions and feelings should not be the sole rule of our lives. One whose life is ruled by emotions is unhappy and makes everyone around him unhappy, too.*

Speaking to newlyweds, Pius XII beautifully described love this way:

"A mutual affection, born solely in the inclination that attracts man towards woman, or even from the mere pleasure for the human gifts which one sex discovers with such satisfaction in the other—such an affection, no matter how beautiful and deep-rooted it may prove to be and no matter how it echoes in the intimacy of the loving conversations of the newly married, would never of itself suffice, nor could it fully achieve that union of your souls which the loving Providence of God has intended and willed when leading you towards each other. Only supernatural love, a bond of friendship between God and man, can tie knots strong enough to resist all the shocks, all the vicissitudes, all the inevitable trials of a long life spent together; only divine grace can make you superior to all the daily miseries, all the multiple contrasts and disparities of tastes or of ideas, springing, like weeds, from the root of weak human nature."

A HARD STRUGGLE

A very active apostolic lay group had taken in a boy who had overcome the drug habit. A Sister very interested in the problem struck up a conversation with him. He was a rugged, soft-spoken boy, obviously not the type to enjoy talking about himself or his experiences. Yet when he spoke of his work with other addicts, he grew enthusiastic.

"It takes one who's been through it to really get to them. That's why I keep at this work—I know they need me."

"And what about your own struggle with the habit?" asked the Sister. "How do you do it?" She wasn't prepared for his straightforward reply:

"With Jesus. I go to Communion every morning. Sister, you could never overcome a habit like this without the strength of Christ. It's a terrific struggle! When I fall once in a while, I don't waste any time running to Him in the sacraments and beginning again!"

The way this boy has overcome a habit that otherwise would have ruined him provides the key for success in other hard struggles. It is no cinch, for instance, for a couple to hold back when strong sexual desires are aroused. Purity involves an almost constant struggle. But the battle must be fought. Breaking God's law before marriage is no way to draw down His blessings on the marriage! Besides, as Pope Pius XII said: "How could one ever hope for chastity and marital fidelity from a young person who could never control himself and master his passions...?"

There is only one way to conquer passion, and that way is *Christ* — with His grace and strength gained through frequent reception of the sacraments.

St. James says: "God resists the proud and gives grace to the humble" (4:6), without which grace, as the Apostle Paul reminds us, nobody can subdue the rebellion of his flesh.

St. Augustine wisely says: "Be subject to God, and your flesh will be subject to you. What is more fitting! What more fair! You are subject to the higher, and the lower is subject to you. Serve Him who made you, so that that which was made for you may serve you."

IF THE FEELING GOES...

Does the first natural physical attraction of a young man and woman develop into lasting love? It can, but real love, mature love does not involve the senses and emotions only; it takes in the intellect and will power as well. It might begin in the senses, but does not stop there. Love of the other person for his own sake becomes a deliberate free act of the will, not ruled solely by emotions. This love is fully aware of the physical attraction and outward charm of the one loved, but it looks beyond this to the person, the character, the very soul hidden beneath outward appearances. When this mature love discovers all that it desires even in the character and personality of the one loved, it becomes concrete and stable. This stable love does not disappear when the sensible feeling goes.

Some married couples panic when they suddenly realize a coldness coming between them. Their senses have reached a saturation point and their feeling for one another begins to wane. Notice it is their *feelings* that begin to lessen. Feeling is not love. A physical attraction is not love. A sensible emotion is not love. True love is more a matter of the will. It is willing the good and happiness of the one loved. To will the other's good and happiness can be done even when no feeling is present, and it *must* be done if the marriage is to be a success.

Mature love has spotted the essential goodness in a person and does not lose sight of this quality even when human failings and faults make themselves evident. Arguments will come and go, some habits will be annoying to the other partner, even disagreements on important matters will cause some anxiety. These things are natural; they will come. But they will be overcome by a love which has its foundation firmly laid in moral qualities rather than in feelings.

Just as a dying fire is revived by adding fuel, the flame of love also can be revived when it has been reduced to a few glowing coals. The fuel for this fire is understanding, small extra acts of kindness, perhaps a little added attention to physical appearance, stepped up interest in the likes of the other, occasional words of affection, a compliment now and then, etc. When two people love each other, it is not difficult to come up with ways and means to please one another.

HAVE "MATCHING" IDEALS

Why not do a little "double checking" during the engagement and just make sure that both of you agree on basic issues?

A seemingly well-adjusted and happily married man was asked at the office one day how he and his wife got along so well. "I decide the major issues and she decides the minor ones," he replied triumphantly. "That's my only secret." "Well," asked one man, still puzzled, "Give us some examples of *minor* issues." "Oh," the other replied, "She decides whether we should rent a house or buy, what school the children should attend, whether she should work or not...etc."

A bit startled, the other pressed still further. "Then, what are the major issues which you decide?"

"Oh, things like who should be the next President...!"

Marriage calls for *real* teamwork. Team members must think alike, especially if God's law is concerned, for then not only virtue but peace of mind and conscience are at stake. Have "matching" ideals in deciding the issues!

Engaged couples must make sure — not just guess or hope — that they both know what marriage is all about. It is important to know, for instance, that if one were to marry with the condition that the other party could not claim the right to have relations in the normal manner, the marriage would be invalid, because a condition would be placed which is contrary to the essential purpose of marriage, namely the procreation of children.

ABOUT HEALTH...

Is it permissible to marry and raise a family if one does not have very good health?

A man and woman who are able to perform the marriage act but are not too healthy could be advised not to marry, but if they should marry, they would not commit any sin. And once married, they have the right to perform the marriage act, as every couple has, even if the children born of them are not strong. Is it not true that many great statesmen and great saints have been people of poor health?

May the State prohibit people afflicted with a disease from marrying?

No. The State cannot forbid those who might have weak or defective children from marrying and raising a family. However, the State may justly urge the engaged couple to undergo a medical examination so that the prospective bride and groom may know the condition of each other's health. If, however, as a result of this examination, the State should forbid the couple to marry, such a prohibition would not be binding on the consciences of Catholics. Thus, for example, the law which states that a person with a venereal disease may not marry has no binding force on the consciences of Catholics, because in all matters that directly concern marriage itself, the State is powerless in the eyes of God.

With regard to the moral problems concerning the "Rh" factors, Pope Pius XII said: "Blood tests are advisable and may be obligatory in certain cases. Carriers may be advised against marriage but may not be forbidden to marry. Married couples who become aware that they have the disease may be advised not to have children but cannot be forbidden to have them. Such a hereditary disease is not sufficient to render a marriage invalid. The death of the first child due to 'Rh' factors is not sufficient to render a marriage null and void."

It is clear, however, that for the sake of the future family, a boy or girl should consider the health aspect when thinking of possible partners.

Is it wrong to limit the number of children because of the mother's health?

It could be permissible to space the frequency of births and limit the number of children if the method used is proper and certain conditions are fulfilled. (This will be discussed in detail later on in this book.)

FOREVER DOES NOT MEAN "IF"

An old story tells of a man and his wife — both good Catholics — who had reached a point where they felt they simply could not get along together any more. They decided they would have to get a divorce. So off they went to call on their pastor and explain the situation to him.

"Can we have a divorce and be free to marry again, Father? Is there any way this can be done?"

"Certainly!" replied the priest. "We can attend to that right away. Just follow me."

Delighted, the couple followed their pastor into another room. He took the holy water sprinkler in his hand, said some prayers (which they could not understand), sprinkled the wife with holy water and then rapped her sharply on the head. The husband, too, was sprinkled and then rapped sharply on the head. Whereupon, the priest began his prayers again and proceeded as before.

The man and his wife stood there stiffly, holding out patiently in view of the longed-for divorce which this unusual ceremony was to bring about. However, after several rounds of blows, their patience began to wear thin, and at last the husband ventured, "Father, how long will this ceremony last?"

"Until one of you dies."

a love for always

When people say they are in love, they mean it "for always." To talk about "love for a limited amount of time" —

or even to admit the possibility of a time limit — is to bring in calculations that negate love.

Couples do not entrust the permanence of their love to chance or circumstances; it is something that is continually achieved through intelligence, will power and effort.

Husband and wife will not let anything else mean more to them than that — neither pride nor freedom nor personal comfort nor even "proving who's right." For true love is always "more right." It excuses everything, believes everything, hopes everything, and puts up with everything.

This is the love that God blesses, consecrates and aids with the sacrament of Matrimony, and Jesus confirms as eternal. It is for the good of husbands and wives, for the spiritual and physical welfare of children, and for the good of society, that God has decreed that the marriage bond can be broken only by death.

No human authority, religious or civil, can break up what the spouses have joined with the intervention of God. Not even the Church can do it.

Charles Cardinal Journet of Switzerland addressed Vatican Council II and the world thus: "The Church's teaching on the indissolubility of marriage is the doctrine of Christ Himself as revealed to us in the Gospel: 'What God has joined together, let no man put asunder.' This doctrine was followed regularly in the early Church. Whatever the practice may have been in certain areas, the doctrine of the Church has always remained unchanged. The Church has no right to change what is of divine law."

If a man or woman about to be married makes an agreement to get a divorce in case of unhappiness, such a condition invalidates the marriage because it is contrary to the nature of matrimony, which is indissoluble. On this point the Church can never change her mind. She can never "swing to the modern trend" because the indissolubility of marriage is not a law of her making.

In a so-called "annulment," the Church only recognizes the fact that a certain marriage was not validly celebrated; it can never break up a valid marriage. Much less can the *State* break up the sacrament, even if it permits divorce.

A couple will think of their love in terms of absolute fidelity, without ever admitting or accepting the idea of its coming to an end.

THE SUPREME GIFT OF MARRIAGE —
CHILDREN

Marriage is one of the most serious commitments between two human beings, characterized by *unity* (the two become one) and *indissolubility* (until death separates them). It is a promise by which the partners pledge to each other things that are most intimate, sacred and enduring. It is a dedication to a cause which rises high above many of the other causes embraced by men.

This cause is the procreation, upbringing, education and comprehensive care of children. Children are the hope of the Church, the nation, the world. Hence, the seriousness of the ceremony whereby two persons announce before the world their readiness, if God grants them children, to assume responsibility for their future.

This teaching, as old as the Gospel and as new as Vatican Council II is reaffirmed in the *Constitution on the Church in the Modern World:*

"Marriage and conjugal love are by their nature ordained toward the begetting and educating of children. Children are really the supreme gift of marriage and contribute substantially to the welfare of their parents. The God Himself who said, 'It is not good for man to be alone' (Gen. 2:18) and 'who made man from the beginning male and female' (Mt. 19:4), wishing to share with man a certain special participation in His own creative work, blessed male and female, saying: 'Increase and multiply' (Gen. 1:28)."

An engaged couple should question one another frankly on their thinking regarding their duty of accepting the children God will send them. They must come to a clear understanding on this fundamental point. And it is clear that if there is no serious will to obey the law of God, it is necessary to break the engagement; better heartbreak than transgression of the sacred duties of matrimony. Better to suffer before than afterwards in a much more bitter manner.

The family must be founded with mature reflection, with clear comprehension of the fact that one is embracing a real mission.

When couples honestly agree on all these "basic issues," the foundation of their married life will rest on solid ground.

PREPARATIONS FOR THE WEDDING

The couple should go to see the pastor at least three months before the wedding. This gives Father the necessary time to make arrangements. It is always better, and a sign of courtesy, to make the church arrangements first before planning the whole wedding.

Customs surround us in every aspect of our lives. Weddings are no exception. It has always been the custom for the wedding itself and the reception to be planned and paid for by the bride's family.

But the groom, too, has duties and expenses which must be met before the great day.

1. The wedding ring or wide gold band has to be purchased.

2. The marriage license should be gotten ahead of time. Some states require a "waiting period," a matter of several hours or even days. (Both husband and wife-to-be must find out ahead of time about the documents required by the Church also, and allow sufficient time to procure those kept in their city of birth or in towns they formerly lived in.)

3. The future groom must choose the best man and ushers, advising them of the type of wedding and attire. He should buy them each a gift to be presented at the bachelor dinner or the night of the wedding rehearsal.

4. If the wedding is larger, he should compile a guest list of family and friends.

5. He should provide the offering which the best man will give to the priest.

6. He pays for the bride's bouquet and boutonnieres for himself and his best man.

7. He orders telephone, electricity and other services which the couple will need upon moving into their new apartment or home.

8. He gives the wedding license and ring to the best man on the wedding day.

9. The groom pays for the entire honeymoon trip.

AND THEN THERE WERE "THREE"

While they may be on the very threshold of marriage, the engaged couple are not yet married.

The young man, while showing himself affectionate and attentive, must continue also to be thoughtful and respectful toward his future wife who, because of her feminine nature, is more refined and sensitive in love, and feels less pressure from the senses. Thus, he will win her greater admiration.

The girl, on the other hand, must not compete in audacity with her fiance. While giving her heart completely to him, she must remain reserved in her demonstrations of affection. In this way she will render herself more desirable on the day of their wedding.

The betrothed can kiss one another with warmth, but not recklessly. Their kiss is a promise—a seal on a love which must last a lifetime. The echo of that kiss must remain unsullied even when years multiply responsibilities and responsibilities bring troubles.

The seal of that kiss must never be broken even when age or sickness steals youth and vigor from it. For that kiss is a commitment to a lifetime of love—the kind of love which supersedes the mere follies of our fickle human emotions. This true and beautiful human love transcends the natural, the base, the earthy.

Thus, Christ shares in your love, makes it permanent and lasting, and you become "three" on life's road.

A DAY TO BE REMEMBERED

4

The Church makes the Wedding Day as blessed, as meaningful as possible, a never-to-be-forgotten day.

On the great day, the Wedding Day, the Church shows her care and love for her sons and daughters about to enter the married state. She makes the day as blessed, as meaningful as possible, a never-to-be-forgotten day. She gives the bride and groom instruction and inspiration in the solemnities with which she surrounds the ceremony, and she provides them with abundant graces taken from the very heart of Christ and bestowed throughout the liturgy of the day.

A couple will be careful not to let the preparations, possible delays in the obtaining of documents or other such difficulties make the pre-wedding period or *the wedding day itself* hectic and nerve-wracking. This would destroy the interior serenity which alone allows a bride and groom to experience the full beauty and happiness of the great event.

Annoyance and frayed nerves can be avoided by planning and punctuality, and by refusing to permit an invasion of photographers or salesmen or the intrusion of other purely external preoccupations.

The wedding celebration itself should especially be protected against distractions. It calls for the recollection due such a great sacrament. The Eucharistic Sacrifice and Holy Communion will frame it in the holiest and most fitting manner and give a truly Christian tone to the promises, best wishes, joy and love.

Because of the excitement and nervousness of the moment, much of the ceremonial significance passes over the young bride and groom. Aware of this, one pastor initiated an unusual and original practice in his parish. He tapes the whole wedding ceremony for each couple he marries and presents them with this precious record of their solemn vows to each other! "When the going becomes hard," he tells them, "play this tape and recall the joys of this day, together with the obligations you assumed and the special helps God promised you. It will cheer you up, I assure you!" (Why not do the same yourselves, on your wedding day?)

As they are about to enter into a union which is most sacred and most serious, in which God, the Creator, will give them a share in the greatest work of creation, it is on their knees, before the altar of God, that the bride and groom pronounce their vows, the "I do" of their sincere reciprocal donation. Here they begin their noble role as "instruments of God" in the great mission of giving to the world "a new man" and bringing him up.

When Jesus came upon this earth, He blessed the newly wedded couple at Cana of Galilee, restored marriage to its pristine height, and made it sacred. And, for His believers, He raised it to the dignity of a sacrament. That is why St. Paul calls matrimony "a holy thing" — a "great sacrament" (Eph. 5:31-32).

Christ referred to the love of marriage to describe His own love for His Church, that is, for the People of God whom He redeemed by His own blood. And so He gave to Christians a new vision of what married life ought to be, a life of self-sacrificing love like His own. It is for this reason that the apostle St. Paul clearly states that marriage is now and for all time to be considered a great mystery, intimately bound up with the supernatural union of Christ and the Church, which union is also to be its pattern.

THE BRIDE'S PRAYER

Lord, grant that I may be worthy of him who has chosen me to be his bride. Lord, grant that I may correspond to the trust of his name and provide for the needs of his house. Lord, grant that I may repay his love with a lifetime of faithfulness.

Because he has chosen me as his companion throughout life, give me the strength to walk at his side for the whole length of the way. And because he has selected me as the sister of his destiny, make me the sharer of all his hours of fatigue and happiness; but reserve for me the greater part of every pain. And because he has chosen me as the mother of his children, infuse in my soul the necessary strength to be always the support, the joy and the peace of his home.

Thus may I become for him the smile and the hope, the refuge and the certainty in the routine of our daily life. In our home today, tomorrow and always, render

*me worthy of my position as friend, wife and mother.
In every hour of sunshine and storm, grant that I may
always work for the happiness of him whom I love.*

THE GROOM'S PRAYER

*My God, on this great day I kneel before You
at the dawn of a new life.*

*I tremble…when faced with the realization of the
lofty commitment which I take upon myself. Ahead
of me lies a life of love joined to the woman I have
chosen. I pledge to You fidelity, devotion
and service to her and to the children You will
send us. By myself I am not capable of this honored
task but Your help and grace will conquer all.*

*Never as today have I felt Your divine
presence. I need Your presence. Make me the man
You expect me to be. Mold me into another Joseph.
Make me resemble that silent and just Husband of
Mary. Give me a pure love and noble sentiments, a love
as true as Adam and Eve's before sin tainted paradise.*

*Give me a love for her which extends far beyond
myself, which is not limited or measured by days,
weeks and years. May it never fade when age and
infirmities rob us of youth. Give us both an
understanding of higher things; and make that
knowledge blossom into wisdom.*

*In joy, in sorrow, in triumph, in failure, I choose
this woman for my queen, my friend, my support, my
other self, until death, and even beyond…for death
will not quench my love.*

*Bless our home with Your sacred presence. Give us
the joy which You left with that unknown couple
at Cana in Galilee. Two lives this day are knitted
into one. Together we will love and cherish the
family You send us. Together we will present
ourselves to you at the journey's end. Make us,
O my God, the couple You expect us to be. Walk
with us through life and heaven will begin right here
on earth. Thank You for creating the woman
I love; thank You for giving her to me. Amen.*

When married couples begin their life together on their knees to beg God's blessings, the proof of His never-failing help in sealing their hearts in love is often very touching.

A husband and wife, both over eighty, are still "on their knees" together each morning at Mass. Despite the fact that she has cancer of the mouth and he can hardly walk from his many infirmities, they manage to make it to Mass, each helping the other along. Even on their way up to the communion rail, the wife will turn back every few steps to make sure the husband is still coming along. No one can see them together without reflecting on the enduring power of love when couples constantly beg God's blessings.

A PAUSE AND A PROMISE

Couples about to marry will no doubt find themselves bombarded with advice. Oh, it will cover a wide gamut of topics, and some opinions will be on the border line of the ridiculous.

But, after all is said, and before anything is done, why not pause and resolve to live your life the best way possible, with one hundred percent effort and good will? That's quite a large promise, true. But, there is one way to stick to your resolution for a lifetime — *Mary*, the Mother given us by God Himself.

Lovers of Mary find it so much easier to please God and to remain good. They let her do the directing of their lives. And she certainly knows what she's doing!

Parents with devotion to our Lady (who knows what it is to be a mother) find many consoling surprises along life's way. When bills are high, and the children are howling, and the neighbors are full of complaints, they call on Mary and things change.

Then, as the years melt away and old age comes on, even though someone may be alone, there is no fear, no trembling, no despair, for life has been lived with Mary.

This, then, is a piece of advice which includes much more: Build your future life on Mary.

Part Two

MARRIAGE— GOD'S OWN INVENTION

"BEGINNING AT THE BEG

1

"The intimate partnership of married life and love has been established by the Creator and qualified by His laws, and is rooted in the conjugal covenant of irrevocable personal consent" (Constitution on the Church in the Modern World, n. 48).

NEWLYWEDS

A woman who was celebrating her fifteenth wedding anniversary confided to me: "The best compliment I get is from people who think Bob and I are newlyweds!"

Yes, mature, faithful love produces familiarity and confidence, and therefore the best of married people have always used many reciprocal acts of love in their marriage — truly affectionate acts of love. They have not disdained to "stoop" to these little signs of affection, so essential for the preservation of conjugal love and necessary to blend their souls in a harmony which is never shattered by the inevitable differences of character.

Once united in marriage, newlyweds must cultivate their love of each other, understanding that their own happiness consists in making their partner happy. Basically, the husband should remember that he has married *a woman*, and the wife, on the other hand, remember that she has married *a man*, and each treat the other accordingly.

Hence, the happiness of the woman requires that the husband give her attention; the wife, in turn, will yield to and satisfy the desires of her husband in order to keep him at home and insure peace.

MARRIAGE BEGINS WHEN THE HONEYMOON FAILS

Happiness in marriage does not automatically come from the mere act of getting married. It does not just settle over the apartment like a great pink cloud. *It is the result of mutual effort, work and sacrifice.* Difficulties have to be expected when two people are living together in the most intimate manner for a lifetime.

74

How very unrealistic for newlyweds to imagine that marriage is one long, romantic honeymoon. Soon enough the stardust will be knocked out of their eyes and they will wake up to find the other not quite so perfect as he or she thought. As one wit commented: *"Marriage begins only after the honeymoon fails."*

This is the time for a rebirth of love. Take into consideration that the past experience (including family, friends, social class, work, education) of each partner has built a particular idea of how a husband or wife ought to be and ought to act. It takes a *realist* to adjust to and love one's partner the way he or she really is with all his or her foibles and faults.

One young wife, looking back over five "rough though happy years" of wedded life admitted that most of her troubles and disillusionments came about because *she did not accept reality.* There was such a difference between how she expected things to be and how they actually turned out. Yet the experience of marriage proved to be much fuller and more meaningful than she had ever dreamed. Of course, as she readily explained, she had to be willing to learn to grow up.

"GETTING TO KNOW YOU"

By reflecting on their own moods, interests and dispositions, on their need for encouragement and affection, couples can better understand each other's reactions and needs. Taking advantage of every opportunity to better know one's partner helps greatly in making one's married life a steady progress in companionship and love.

Telling each other their feelings, aspirations, fears and sorrows will promote understanding and love — that familiar, trusting love that must unite a couple if they are to be each other's comfort and support in the inevitable trials and hard knocks of married life. Says the *Constitution on the Church in the Modern World,* "Sealed by mutual faithfulness and hallowed above all by Christ's sacrament, this love remains steadfastly true in body and in mind, in bright days or dark" (n. 49).

BE A GOOD HOME "CONVERSATIONALIST"

How to start a good conversation? One way for newlyweds is by relating the day's happenings — pleasant, humorous or annoying as they may be. As confidence in each other grows, more delicate points will be touched upon — their families, their occasional irritation with each other, even defects and errors they once hid. All this will bring about greater understanding and sympathy, not ridicule or indifference.

After a while each will get to know when the other wants to get something off his or her mind. *Then* is the moment to listen, even if dinner gets cold or sleep is delayed.

To ignore the other's impulse to talk is to take a step backwards in their relationship. It will be a little harder for the partner to confide the next time. Eventually mutual trust will weaken and confidences will be given to outsiders — she to mother or girlfriends, he to the fellows at work; or worse, husband and wife may begin to confide in those who could be an occasion of sin....

A certain couple were thought to be an "ideal pair" by their neighbors and acquaintances. Then suddenly the wife walked out, and the husband, alone and heartbroken, ashamed at what people were thinking, admitted to a close friend: "For years now our private life together has been torture, even though we kept up the outward appearance. We never could sit down and *talk* pleasantly together."

According to him, his wife gave him no peace with her constant criticism. (Naturally there are always two sides to every quarrel, but we relate this man's story for the lesson it offers to future brides.) "If I were a bit late to come up from the cellar for supper, she'd spend the whole meal complaining. She found fault with everything I did, picking on me over and over again for the least little thing. Why, for just breaking a cup handle, she'd "start in" as if I were a baby.

"What most got me — and she knew it — was her insulting remarks about my family and relatives. How many times she'd yell: 'You're just like your father!' Or, 'You're acting just like that brother of yours!' The direct insults I could take, but the constant cracks about my family got me so angry that I usually tried to avoid these occasions as much as possible. As soon as I got home from work, I'd go right down into the cellar to work and I'd stay there as long as I could. There was just no more communication between us!"

Avoiding words or actions which annoy or hurt one's partner goes a long, long way toward building a happy marriage, as does the rendering of little services without being asked. The man who works overtime to give Betty and the children a much-needed vacation shows he really loves

his family; the wife who, even after a long day of washing and ironing, makes an extra effort to cook her husband's favorite dish shows how much she cares for him. One husband drove his family from North Carolina to Massachusetts in one day in order to visit relatives. Asked by his hosts how long the trip took, he nonchalantly stated, "Just nineteen hours."

"And you drove the whole distance by yourself?"

"Sure."

"Didn't your wife take the wheel for a few hours?"

"Oh no!" the man exclaimed. "I wouldn't think of asking her to drive. She had only three hours of sleep last night and besides she has the baby to take care of." And this pair are not newlyweds, but have been married over twenty years.

CALL A "FAMILY COUNCIL"

Wise couples agree on all basic issues and on most small ones. Sharing decision-making, experience and responsibilities and enjoying it contributes greatly to the happiness of marriage. In fact, the more sharing of activities and the more agreement on fundamental issues there is, the more harmonious will wedded life be.

Happy the husband and wife who take an interest in each other's pastimes and hobbies.

One young husband related, "Every anniversary Dotty and I exchange presents; this is not too different, but our presents are. I happen to be a very enthusiastic shutter-bug, but dropped it when I realized that it didn't interest Dot. Well, on the eve of our first anniversary, she amazed me by setting up the camera, and taking a picture of a still-life composition, using lights and shadow effectively.

"While the prints were developing, she smiling wished me happy anniversary and concluded, 'This is my anniversary gift to you!' Unknown to me, she had been studying photography.

"Dotty had always enjoyed dancing, whereas I thought it was foolish. But during the following year I secretly took lessons and as we danced together on our second anniversary, I whispered, 'I hope you like my present, dear.'"

FAITH...REALISM...SACRIFICE

Married love, lived in faith and realism and sprinkled throughout with genuine sacrifice, will one day be perfected in the glory of the Father in heaven. This is explained so pertinently by the *Constitution on the Church in the Modern World,* which says: "Authentic married love is caught up into divine love and is governed and enriched by Christ's redeeming power and the saving activity of the Church, so that this love may lead the spouses to God with powerful effect and may aid and strengthen them in the sublime office of being a father or a mother" (n. 48).

No human building...

"Marriage and the family are not the work of men alone, not a human building produced and dominated in its inner being by historical conditions and those of environment, and changeable as these. Marriage and the family come from God. They are God's work and they answer to an essential design which God Himself has mapped out and which surpasses the changeable conditions of the times, continuing always unchanged. It is God who by these means wishes to render man a sharer in His highest prerogatives, in His love for men and His faculty of creating life. For this reason marriage and the family have a transcendent relationship with God. From Him they proceed and to Him they are ordained. Families are founded on earth and live there at first but are destined to reassemble in heaven.

"Any conception or doctrine which does not sufficiently recognize this essential relationship of marriage and the family with its divine origin and destiny surpassing human experience, would fail to understand its deeper reality and would be unable to find the correct solutions to its problems" (Paul VI).

Marriage, as one columnist put it, is not for little boys and girls who "think they're going to make a go of it with candy hearts." Marriage is for mature men and women who are ready to give their all to build a successful wedded life.

Don't Make In-Laws "Out-Laws"

All of a sudden newlyweds are faced with something different: in-laws. Each of the spouses has inherited another whole family, father and mother-in-law and brothers and sisters-in-law. It's really quite wonderful, you know, for just as his family is the greatest in the whole wide world, hers is too. So, nobody loses and everybody wins!

The story is told of a young bride who went with her husband to visit his family the first Sunday after they were married.

The bride noticed that she wasn't making much progress in winning the friendship of her husband's younger sister, who was still single and living at home. Sunday after Sunday they went to visit, and the gap...the personality clash... became an obvious source of uneasiness for both, but especially for the wife. Finally, she confided her problem to her husband. "I love to visit your folks," she said, "if only *she* weren't there." "The best way to cure it," her wise husband advised, "is to keep on going, and to keep trying to make her your friend."

Soon enough a year had passed...and the couple had their first baby. "Let's ask your sister to be the godmother," the good young wife suggested. Her husband liked the idea just fine. His younger sister was so thrilled by the choice that all previous (real or imaginary) differences were fast forgotten, and the two women have been fast friends ever since.

Most of us are familiar with the cartoon picture of mother-in-law and father-in-law as overbearing, interfering individuals who just can't seem to realize that Ellen or Joe is married and on his or her own now. But cartoons are not real; they are exaggerated in order to poke fun. Most in-laws are wonderful people. Mother and father-in-law are responsible for the good and lovable traits in a partner; they have shown their devotion by years of generous self-sacrifice to raise their son or daughter well.

Consequently, when a young couple marry, they become a part of each other's family circle. They become immersed in all sorts of brothers, sisters, uncles, aunts, cousins and so forth. It is only right; in-laws as well as parents have a right to expect some of their love and devotion.

However, let them keep in mind the words of our Lord: "For this cause (matrimony) a man shall leave his father and mother, and cleave to his wife, and the two shall become one flesh" (Matt. 19:5). This means that newlyweds are no longer primarily son or daughter: they are now *husband* and *wife*. Love and esteem for parents should continue to be shown, but their first love, loyalty and devotion belong to their partner.

RUNNING TO MOTHER

If it can possibly be avoided, it is best not to live with the in-laws. Living next door or in the same apartment building is also unwise. This makes it too easy to "run to mother" when things get difficult. The newly married "he" and "she" need privacy to work out difficulties together in order to firmly cement the bond of unity in their marriage. Any problems which might arise should be resolved between them, or, if necessary with professional counselors. They can discuss with each other their family backgrounds, problems and customs, the good and not-so-good points of their parents.

However, couples should never make remarks about each other in front of their parents; otherwise, even after the problem has long since been solved, their parents may still worry about it.

A jolly ninety-six-year old widow remembers with glee many humorous incidents in her married life. As she relates one after another, it is obvious that the good-natured kidding that went on constantly between her husband and her was linked to a deep affection and perfect mutual trust.

"One of my husband's favorite stunts was to arouse my mother's anger by pretending to be critical of me. My mother lived with us and still considered me more *her* daughter than *his* wife. He knew this, but no friction ever developed because of his good humor. Right at dinner, with my mother opposite him, he would begin to scold me, looking thoroughly annoyed with me. My mother would eye him, her cheeks flushing an increasingly deeper red, but she would not be sure if he were really serious. Finally, she would angrily rise to my defense—only to spot the twinkle in his eye or a wink at me.

"I have often thought that if we lived together so serenely, most of the credit was due to my husband's wonderful disposition. (And if we did have something to say to each other, we made sure it was never in front of my mother!)"

Couples should never bring up what in-laws said about them before marriage. If mother or dad had something to say, that "something" should have been evaluated then. If their parent's criticism was accepted as just, then they must simply work out the problem now. If they felt mother's or dad's remarks were uncalled for before the marriage, they should be forgotten now.

SELF-EXAMINATION

If a husband or wife find difficulties between them and their in-laws arising, let them ask themselves if they are taking into account their good intentions and differences in family background, or if they are resentful at having to share the affection of their partner and children with others. There is a great difference between filial love and conjugal love and the heart of every married person is big enough for both.

Let couples take the in-laws' well-intentioned advice (though perhaps intrusive) with patience and understanding and they will reap rich dividends in domestic peace and happiness.

Keep in mind that in-laws often offer much assistance in times of crisis and can be the strongest supporters in days of adversity.

Every affection and gesture of respect offered to one's in-laws is a proof of love for one's partner. And who can measure the joy that floods the heart of "mom" and "dad" in-law when they see that they are loved and wanted. When they offer to help or to buy something, let them.... Let them have that consolation, for they remember too well when they were young and struggling. They were once "newlyweds" too. And be grateful for everything they do. They have generously made room for a new member in their hearts. Match their goodness by sincerely accepting them as well.

LET ME CONSULT ... TH

Various circumstances will determine who should handle the money, whether it be husband or wife, or both. However, there can be no doubt as to the ultimate purpose of the income. No matter who earns it, or manages it, it must be used for the good of the family as a whole.

TWO MASTERS

"No man can serve two masters," Jesus said to His disciples, "for either he will hate the one and love the other, or else he will stand by the one and despise the other. You cannot serve God and mammon. Therefore I say to you, do not be anxious for your life, what you shall eat; nor yet for your body, what you shall put on. Is not the life a greater thing than the food, and the body than the clothing? Look at the birds of the air: they do not sow, or reap, or gather into barns; yet your heavenly Father feeds them. Are not you of much more value than they?" (Mt. 6:24-26)

In the Gospel passage above, our Lord is not saying that money ("mammon" here refers to money) must be completely eliminated and that we must live like the birds of the air. No, *He teaches us that a prudent management of our finances is necessary, but that we shouldn't let the idol of money dominate our lives.*

BUY OR RENT?

Saving, planning, dreaming together from the outset of their engagement makes for the beginning of a long and beautiful life. *Where are we going to live?* is an important question young couples ask each other. There are several factors which help them to decide.

Live in your own apartment or home is oft-heard advice. Even a one room apartment with bath is fine if it is their "own." Then, little by little, they save for that new home. Even if it seems years away, it is worth the effort. No matter how scanty the paycheck is, by dint of good management and sheer practicality, a couple can achieve their goal.

A young housewife, with one small child, and expecting another, writes these following thoughts to her family back home:

"George (her husband) has almost two hours of crazy driving every day. He gets up at 5:30 a.m.; sometimes 4:00 in the winter and during weeks when he has to go in early. Needless to say, a happy, organized home helps. Still wish I could earn something at home to help but he doesn't want me to baby-sit. Oh! we are not that "close" for money but it would be good to be able to do a few little extra things once in a while.

"You know me—I'm as "tight" as ever. But he never complains!...Takes his lunch, I cut his hair, etc. We are no different from most young couples starting out. You have to be ready for emergencies. We have plenty of insurance and have more to show for our efforts than most...."

See what sacrifice and good management can do? And what happiness this couple witnesses as they struggle and work toward a common goal: the good of their family.

Some even manage to scrape together the down payment for a home during the engagement. This, of course, is wonderful, for then hard-earned money can be put into home payments instead of exorbitant rental fees. A reputable real estate broker will advise on the fine points of financing, tax rates, the neighborhood, zoning laws, transportation and other facilities; conveniently located church, school and shopping districts.

Whether buying or renting, experts in the marriage field (graduates of the school of experience) advise selecting the home or apartment before the furniture.

All the effort and personal labor a couple puts into their home and furniture is an *investment* in their own future!

NOT MINE OR YOURS..."OURS"

If both husband and wife know exactly how much income their partnership has and its assets, and avoid all secretiveness between them regarding money matters, many an argument will never occur. It is not the level of income, but stability and security of finances that contribute to the success of a marriage.

By their matrimonial vows husband and wife have agreed to share life together; this means a total and unreserved sharing. Thus no longer is anything "mine" or "yours"; it is *"ours."* Various circumstances will determine who should handle the money, whether it be husband or wife, or both.

However, there can be no doubt as to the ultimate purpose of the income. No matter who earns it, or manages it, it must be used for the good of the family as a whole.

Sometimes one or the other of the partners may forget this. One husband, a chain smoker, seemed unable to cut down on his excessive consumption of cigarettes. His wife pointed out to him that since his pay was moderate and his family numerous, she was having difficulty in making ends meet. If only he would smoke less.... The father tried again to break himself of his excessive smoking, but without success. Then one night he dreamed that he was taking food from his children's mouths. The very suggestion impressed him so deeply that from that day on he never smoked again.

STICKING TO IT

Husband and wife should wisely agree to live according to a pre-arranged budget, but never permit the budget to become so important that failure to follow it leads to disputes between them. This requires self-discipline and compromise on the part of both.

One man thought so highly of his wife's ability that he would turn over his whole paycheck and let her manage the family finances by herself. Even the bank account was in her name only, though he was the only wage-earner.

The wife in this case responded in a manner quite unworthy of her husband's goodness and trust. Five dollars a week was what she gave him, to be used for gas to and from work. And if he asked for more some weeks, for needed car repairs for instance, she never failed to make a scene over it. He had to keep an account of his expenditures and she exploded if he failed to make it sufficiently detailed.

A situation like this certainly cannot promote happiness in marriage. The above couple, in fact, are now separated. Moreover, a short time before she left him, she had sold the house, depositing the money in the bank together with their savings—all in her name only. Her parting act was to withdraw every cent, leaving him literally penniless.

How *should* the finances be handled? This must be worked out by each couple. A good solution is one which works the best for *that* particular couple.

Bill, a cautious, budget-minded individual, does not insist that his wife, Joan, make the same strict accounting of expenses that he makes for himself. Joan, not given to worry about planning and anticipating expenditures, controls her tendency to carefree spending and makes an effort to stick to basic budgeting principles.

Kevin, who manages the money in the Brown family, is considerate of the personal needs of his wife as well as the expenses of the home and gives her enough money each week to cover both. A "saver" by nature, Kevin nonetheless realizes the line is thin between a miser and a careful saver. He desires to have a good amount in the bank for his family's future in case of misfortune or sickness. Yet in order to achieve this goal, he would never permit his wife the humiliation of being without money even for emergencies, nor does he accuse her of being selfish if she wants a little extra to spend on herself.

Martha manages the money in the Smith family. Nonetheless she always discusses with her husband the bills, expenditures and future plans, showing him her interest in his advice.

One husband claimed, "When I found out what good buys Marge could get, I didn't mind letting her handle the money. When she shops she gets almost double the amount of things that I do for the same money. I soon learned how careful she is to put a little aside each week for our children's education."

In general, couples should live according to their means, assuming the least debt possible. Both mother and father should be willing to bear the financial sacrifices, as well as the joys involved in family life. The future of their children should also be provided for.

Domestic economists have figured what proportion of family income can be used to pay off debt without endangering family security. It is inconsiderate and unreasonable for one party to deprive the other of important conveniences (when the debt thus incurred could comfortably be met) just because he or she hates the idea of being in debt.

EASY PAYMENTITIS!

A disease, which is getting to be almost as prevalent as the common cold, is "easy paymentitis." Advertisers display their products in glowing colors and "push" them with rich descriptive terms. The climax of their advertis-

ing pitch comes when they warmly assure the customer, "It's so easy to pay for, just ten dollars down and five dollars a week...." Oh, how much matrimonial happiness has been destroyed by the "easy payment!"

This is not to argue against the use of easy payment — just its *abuse*. Young couples especially can fall prey to the lure of easy payment, although older couples aren't invulnerable either. The stepped-up advertising techniques of our culture can sway young marrieds to believe that they must start their wedded life on the level of living their parents reached only after ten or twelve years of marriage.

One young wife insisted soon after their marriage that they had to have new furniture. "Look, honey," her husband returned, "I know this stuff isn't the best, but with what I make right now, new furniture is out of the question." Unsatisfied and concerned only with her selfish desires, the wife continued to nag and complain that their furnishings were cheap, shabby and so forth. Eventually that marriage ended in divorce — all for a few pieces of furniture!

Let young couples ask themselves, "Do we really *need* this or that item? or is it only a luxury that we can put off getting until a later date or even do without altogether?"

SENSIBLE USE OF CREDIT

Credit plays a very important part in economics. Without it the standard of living would be sharply cut down. However, sensible use of credit requires proper guidance for the average family. The prudent couple will consult an expert in finances (such services can be found at almost any bank) who can advise them how far they can go into debt without endangering their financial security. Once he knows your amount of income, your present debts, your usual domestic expenditures and a few other details (all kept in strict confidence, of course), he can give you valuable suggestions as to your credit commitments.

The following are a few rules of thumb regarding the wise use of credit.

1. You don't get credit for nothing. Lending money costs money and the borrower pays the bill.

It helps to find out the different interest rates available. Even though one per cent doesn't sound like much, over the years and on a large amount, it adds up. Don't confuse the term "finance charges" with "interest rate." Usually state law controls interest rates, which therefore do not vary too much between loan firms. However, the cost of borrowing money or buying on time can go sky high due to service charges, insurance and other "financial charges."

2. Shop with care. Don't let a persuasive salesman talk you into paying more than an item is worth. He wants to sell; you want to make a wise purchase and he isn't going to do your job.

3. Buy from reputable businesses.

4. Read over and make sure you understand any contract before you sign it.

One man figured his car would cost fifty-five dollars a month. Without reading the contract, he signed it and discovered when the bill came that he owed ninety-three dollars a month. He didn't realize that the contract included insurance and other costs, bringing the total to almost twice what he planned to pay.

5. Don't extend your credit beyond what you can afford. Figure your living expenses for a month, subtract that from your total monthly income. The result is the amount which can safely be used for savings and time payments. In fact, the total of installment credit bills should not be more than one week's salary. If the family's weekly income is one hundred twenty, then no more than one hundred twenty dollars' worth of time payments a month should be owed.

6. Put something aside in case of illness, loss of job or other misfortune.

It is also very commendable, if income allows it, for newlyweds to invest in stock, even early in their marriage. This stock will help provide security and pay for their children's education.

7. When buying, take care of *necessities* first, then shop for *wants*.

8. Nobody ever said it was a sin to pay cash.

In fact, you'll find that cash always does the best buying. Try purchasing a car and just see. The dealer will quote one price for cash and a higher one if one wants to trade-in an old car and finance the rest.

HOME FINANCIERS

"You shall not steal!" says the seventh commandment and it refers not only to outright robbery but stealing by refusing to pay one's debts. First of all, it is not honest to take on more debts than one can possibly meet. Desire to enjoy expensive pleasures or to make an impression socially does not justify living beyond one's means. Some people may claim they are unable to pay their bills, but they keep right on purchasing luxuries, thus showing their insincerity.

One rather young father of a good-sized family frequently receives help from charitable groups because they know that his modest salary as a day laborer cannot adequately meet the family's needs. Yet recently this man went out and made a down payment on a new Cadillac!

Just because the creditor can produce no written proof that a just debt was incurred does not relieve the debtor of the moral obligation to make the payment. What may be excused in a court of law will not be excused at the court of God at the Last Judgment.

SPREADING OUT THEIR WEALTH

Money and in-laws can spell out a source of conflict between husband and wife. If Carol's wealthy parents buy her expensive gifts, won't this make her husband, Paul, resentful? It may, but this can be avoided if Carol makes it clear to Paul that the gift is for both of them to use and to enjoy equally.

What about Bob's insistence upon giving financial aid to his widowed sister? Is he being fair to his wife Jean and to his children by so doing? Bob should be commended for helping his needy sister, provided he is not depriving his own family of necessities by doing so. Furthermore, he will always consult Jean before making any contributions to his relatives and, if necessary, will compromise in order to reach an agreement with her.

If marriage is to be a true partnership, as it should be, if both husband and wife have full knowledge of their income and assets, if each one tries (within reason) to follow a budget, there should be little or no friction concerning money spent for recreation, whether shared or alone.

Let the husband realize that he does not have the right to spend as much as he wishes on personal recreation just because he earns the income. Let him resolve to be considerate of his wife's need for recreation and spending money of her own and provide her with opportunities equal to those he wants for himself.

Expenses	food	clothes	doctor and medi-cine	rent	trips and enter-tainment	AUTO-MOVIL car	taxes
ecedente L.							
	4.						
	2.800.						
	1.000.						
	4.100.						
	3.000.						
	2.200.						
	3.200						
	6.000.						

August

Let the wife, for her part, not take advantage of her husband's trust in her by making extravagant purchases or by spending so much time in entertainment and hobbies that her duties as wife and mother are neglected. Let her resolve not to let her husband's reasonable personal expenditures make her resentful as she trusts that he will not resent her personal spending.

When it comes to religious contributions, they should readily agree that the church they attend should receive financial support from them according to their means. If both have the same appreciation for religion, and if their appreciation is deepened and strengthened as the years pass, they will not have difficulty in agreeing how much to give to their church and how best to meet the appeals made by religious organizations. If one of the partners should unfortunately grow lax in the practice of religion, he or she should not try to prevent the other from giving reasonable financial support to the church that still ministers to his or her spiritual needs.

NICK'S JOB

Does Lois have a right to say anything about the type of job Nick takes to earn their bread and butter? Strictly speaking, Lois doesn't. It is up to Nick to pick the kind of work he wants to do.

Nick may be tempted to take on two jobs in order to make extra money. He should ask himself if the extra money is really necessary. If not, is he being fair to deprive Lois and the children of much of his time and possibly the danger to his health by overwork? Wouldn't his family far prefer the attention and companionship of a husband and father rather than a few extra dollars in the kitty?

Lois, on her part, should encourage Nick in his work, move willingly if his job requires a transferral from one city to another, and do the best she can to make home a happy, harmonious place. Lois can suggest, if it seems necessary, that Nick look for or take better employment than he has. Above all, she must never nag him because he doesn't earn enough to meet her wants or insist that he take a job for which he has neither aptitude nor inclination.

Far more than she may realize, a husband depends on his wife for support and encouragement in his work. The late Fritz Kreisler, upon hearing himself lauded for "distinguished and exceptional service" as a violinist and citizen, turned toward his wife Harriet and declared: "Without the constant guidance, advice and help of my dear wife...I would not have achieved one-half of the things I am said to have achieved."

Money in marriage is like water. Too little causes hardship. A moderate amount or a great amount used well is fine. But a great amount or a moderate amount abused can be disastrous.

Thus couples will do well before they are married or soon afterward, to establish certain wise principles together upon which they will make monetary decisions so that the financial stream of their married life will flow along smoothly.

Above all, while doing the things that have to be done every day, they will try to enjoy as much leisure time together, and with their children, as they can.

Only in this way does the family grow closer and closer and, as a consequence, happier and happier.

THAT WORKING WOMAN

To work or not to work—that is the question. In general, unless economic necessity demands it, a wife should not work outside the home.

Yes, that working woman, who is also a wife and mother, is quite a familiar sight in office and factory today. In fact, official reports say that for the first time in the history of the nation, married women outnumber single women in the work force.

Well, *to work or not to work; that is the question.* In general, unless economic necessity demands it, a wife should not work outside the home. And statistics show that only one married woman in seven is the only source of income for the family. Therefore, most married women work to maintain the family at a higher level of living than can be attained on the husband's pay alone. A smaller, but sizable portion of married women seek employment as a source of creative satisfaction which they are unable to find in the home. A few work in order to be independent of their husbands or to be free from the relative seclusion of their homes.

One mother of six deeply regrets the many years she worked without, she admits, a *real* need for doing so. "I beg my children," she often says, "to forgive me for what I deprived them of by deserting them to the care of babysitters so that we could have more 'things' in our lives. I was a misguided mother!"

A girl and boy soon to be married were talking to a friend. The bride-to-be, who had been working for two years since her graduation from high school, was asked: "Are you going to keep working after you're married?"

"Oh no!" came the quick reply. And then she added with obvious pleasure, smiling up at her fiancé, "*He* doesn't want me to."

What about the argument that an interesting job is better than staying at home, secluded and lonely — especially when the family is small?

"Me? Get lonely?" one young wife repeated in surprise. "Why, between cleaning and washing and cooking and keeping the house looking cheery and attractive, I don't have any time weighing on my hands!" And her house is really homey, warm and inviting always. No wonder her husband loses no time in getting home after work! And friends of this couple make no secret of the fact that they like to drop in often. The wife's love for and pride in her home, even though it is an old house, has worked wonders.

If for a few hours a day a woman devotes her talents to some aspect of her previous job, this is stimulating and while it helps the family, it certainly does not steal from her total gift as wife and mother.

Taking in typing, some home secretarial work, addressing envelopes, selling cosmetics, tutoring, piano lessons, babysitting, ironing, sewing, knitting, etc. — some time can be devoted to these. It is so easy to create a demand for "home services." Mother can advertize in the local paper, or just tell the club girls. News travels very fast as we all know. And the work will come steadily in. Mom will be using her past skills and talents daily to help the family and to broaden her own horizons.

HOW MUCH SHALL WE BARTER?

Many newlyweds desire, as is natural, to start off their married life with the best. Therefore the young bride continues to work in order to help pay for the new house, furniture and car. Both enjoy fine clothes and club memberships.

However, for material goods, husband and wife sometimes barter many things and risk losing their happiness.

First of all, a young man should ask himself if it is right to propose marriage when his present income cannot support two people at a decent standard of living. He should consider whether or not his earnings will be enough to provide for several children as God permits them to come.

When the wife works, she is pressed for time to do the housework and frequently cannot even prepare decent meals. The husband, who according to nature is supposed to be the head of the family and its breadwinner, feels a loss of dignity. One woman even asked her husband how far he would have gotten if it weren't for her earnings. Are extra comforts and luxuries worth the husband's possible loss of self-respect? This situation creates tension which may cause grave problems later on.

Furthermore the young wife is attractive. There may well be advances from other men in her place of employment. Because of our weak human nature, troublesome situations can arise.

Then comes the day when the wife finds she is expecting. Abruptly the income is cut, but payments on car, house, and furniture still have to be met. Added to the difficulty in paying these bills may be the resentment of the wife — either against her husband because he cannot continue to support her in the manner she desires or against the unborn child which has caused the slash in income.

Thus husband and wife will be prudent enough to consider any wifely earnings as temporary and not do any long range planning on the basis of two paychecks.

WORKING FOR THE "EXTRAS"

When the wife works, the temptation to defer having children or to practice birth control can be very strong. The wife may claim she would like to have children, but "I just can't afford to give up my job." If in reality she is working not to provide necessities, but *extras*, then she is trading the proper fruit of marriage — children — for material advantages. And the marriage itself may be endangered.

It is interesting to note that the chances of divorce seem to decrease with children. In fact, the lowest divorce rate is found among couples with four or more children. Youngsters in the home help to cement the marriage bond. Mother and father have new lives to nourish, protect and guide; with all their interest and devotion centered around their family, the chances of their giving in to selfishness and pettiness lessen considerably.

A HOME WITHOUT A MOTHER
IS JUST
AN EMPTY HOUSE

What about the working woman with children? Statistics show there are approximately two million children under the age of six and three million children between the ages of six and twelve whose mothers work full time. How can we *overlook* the connection between the increase of

juvenile delinquency and family break-ups and the rising number of mothers holding full-time jobs?

Children need maternal love and care especially when they are small. Babysitters, nurses, relatives, day nurseries are no substitute for a mother and do not relieve her of her responsibilities as a parent.

The good mother puts her children's happiness and welfare above her desire for material conveniences. She realizes that the sense of security a child receives from parental attention and care will contribute immensely toward his future emotional maturity and ability to stand up under strain. She knows that few things terrify a child more than the feeling of being abandoned. The insecurity felt by children who have lost their mothers early in life is sometimes never overcome. In fact, emotional disturbances which come up in a person's later life frequently were germinated in a childhood lacking maternal interest and attention.

Even mothers who are forced by necessity to work outside the home must do all they can to make their maternal presence felt. One girl recalls how her mother left for work only after they were home from school, and late at night when returning from work she would go around to each of the children's beds. They remember half waking up to hug her and feel her loving kiss and then happily falling asleep again. They never doubted that only real necessity forced her to go out to work.

TEENS TOO NEED MOM'S HELP

Even when her children become teenagers, the dedicated mother sees their need, not so much for bodily care, as for love, sympathy and companionship. She knows how they look forward to seeing her after school, even if all they say is "Hi!" A home without a mother is just an empty house. What teenager cares to come home to four walls with a roof when his or her heart is full of desires, hopes and fears that yearn to be expressed? What they need more than any material comforts are attention and guidance in those years when they are struggling to be self-assured and grown-up, yet are so immature and insecure. Teens are thinking about their future and they need mom's help in making a wise decision.

A working mother is usually too busy between a job and housework to be able to give her sons and daughters all the

help and advice they need. She may well be too busy to in-
quire carefully into their friendships, their social life, their
ways of having fun. Rushing off to work, she may quickly give
son or daughter permission to go to a party or on a date without knowing any of the particulars. Chaperoned or unchaper-
oned party? Where? With whom? Did she ever meet the boy
or girl her teen is going out with? While young people may be
naturally good, they are also naturally weak. When parental
supervision is lacking, it is only too easy for them to fall into
bad habits and delinquency.

The mother who wants the best for her teens knows that
if they find in her a sympathetic, attentive listener, they will
be much less apt to go elsewhere for advice and companionship. She may want them to have spending money, extra
clothes, money for special activities which she could supply
by working. But she knows that they can earn some money
on their own. Babysitting jobs, newspaper routes, lawn mow-
ing, part-time work in a store—in all these ways and many
more, teens can earn their own money and at the same time
learn the value of a dollar!

"WAGE TAG" ON A WOMAN

A few years back a prominent figure spoke publicly
about the need of industry and government for women's
services. Married women were asked to make their contribution also. Commenting on such an outlook, Rev. Edward L.
Murphy, S.J. remarked: "To put a wage tag on a married
woman as proof of her value to national life or as proof of
democracy ignores both the primacy of the spiritual in
woman's nature and the need of ordered marriage and family
life in this nation."

The wise woman, considerate of her husband's happiness,
knows she may put a strain on their relations by being em-
ployed full time outside the home. By nature the husband is
fitted to lead the family and provide for its needs. The qualities a woman must develop in order to succeed in the world
of work differ much from those which make her a success in
the home. Thus she does not complement the qualities of her
husband as nature intended, but is inclined to compete with
him. And her husband may well resent the lack of attention
he receives since much of her time is occupied with her job.

Recent investigations reveal that homes where both husband and wife bring in paychecks show an increase in tension. Needless to say, money is one of the chief sources of friction, as well as domestic management and sharing of household tasks. It is especially when the wife works against the husband's will that the ship of their marriage is headed for dangerous waters.

The working mother herself is bound to worry about her children at home, particularly if one of them is sick. The pressure to fulfill the demands of her job and at the same time give proper attention to her family causes a conflict in the mother and can easily produce in her a sense of guilt. Striving conscientiously to meet the requirements of both positions may exhaust her physically as well as mentally. Then how can she be her best self in the company of her husband and children? How can she fit Pius XII's description of a mother?—"the sun of the family by the light of her smile and the warmth of her word—smile and word which inspire, mold and soften the soul. One glance from her eyes throws a light with a thousand reflections; one sound from her lips contains a thousand words of affection. Such light and sound spring from a mother's heart, create and enliven the paradise of childhood, radiate everywhere goodness and gentleness even when they upbraid and reprove, so that young souls, who feel more deeply, may understand more intimately and profoundly the laws of love."

MOM'S WORKING DOLLAR

According to economic studies, the mother's paycheck does not really add that much to the family's income. It is estimated that for every dollar earned by the mother, the total income increases by only sixty cents. The other forty cents has to cover transportation, lunches, personal needs required by employment and of course, increased taxes. Also, the working mother does not have time to do many things within the home that save money. Health may suffer from quickly prepared and poorly planned meals. Less tension in the family might eliminate some of those high medical bills. Sometimes expensive means of recreation are considered indispensable by those who are trying to relax from overwork.

Recently a sister-superior whose Order runs a child day-care nursery observed: "I am convinced that a working mother does not save a cent! She has so many added expenses. First, she must pay the nursery. Then, she must purchase a second car, for generally she and her husband work in different locations. That new car requires upkeep—gas, repairs, insurance. Next, a stylish wardrobe is expensive to buy and to maintain. Imagine the dry cleaning bill. When it comes to meals, mom needs something quick. She cannot make use of left-overs and other thrifty means. Thus, she resorts to 'take-out' or 'TV' dinners. She probably even has a cleaning lady once a week.

"Is it worth it?" Sister queried. "Our tots run from ages two to five. Some arrive as early as seven o'clock in the morning and are not picked up until six at night. How pitiful! They barely know their parents. What a deep void it will cause in their precious childhood days!"

Every real man wants to earn the living, but he needs his wife to make life worth the living. Behind every successful man is a good woman inspiring, tantalizing and tranquilizing him.

Good Pope John XXIII once said: "Within the walls of the home let there be that ardor of charity which existed amid the family at Nazareth. Let all Christian virtues flourish, unity reign, examples of the good life shine forth."

SEX AND THE TRANSMISSIO

Sex is a privileged gift which God intended to be used only in marriage, enabling husband and wife to bring the pure love they had for each other before marriage to a perfect completion in the sacrament of Matrimony.

A young couple in their first year of marriage were entertaining another couple about their own age. The guests both remarked on the presence of religious articles and pictures here and there in the tastefully decorated apartment. At the same time they made it clear that they themselves had grown quite cool toward the Church.

"The Church puts a damper on the pleasures of marriage," declared the husband. "She doesn't let you enjoy being married, when it comes to the aspect of sex."

The other couple both registered surprise at that. "Oh, no!" exclaimed the wife. "It's just the opposite. Reading and following what the Church teaches on married love has deepened our joy and really made everything richer in meaning for us!"

Just what does the Church teach about sex in marriage? We listen first to Vatican II:

"Many men of our age highly regard true love between husband and wife as it manifests itself in a variety of ways....

"This love is an eminently human one since it is directed from one person to another through an affection of the will; it involves the good of the whole person, and therefore can enrich the expressions of body and mind with a unique dignity, ennobling these expressions as special ingredients and signs of the friendship distinctive of marriage. This love God has judged worthy of special gifts, healing, perfecting and exalting gifts of grace and of charity. Such love, merging the human with the divine, leads the spouses to a free and mutual gift of themselves, a gift providing itself by gentle affection and by deed; such love pervades the whole of their lives: indeed by its busy generosity it grows better and grows greater. Therefore it far excels mere erotic inclination, which, selfishly pursued, soon enough fades wretchedly away.

"This love is uniquely expressed and perfected through the marital act. The actions within marriage by which the couple are united intimately and chastely are noble and worthy ones. Expressed in a manner which is truly human,

these actions promote that mutual self-giving by which spouses enrich each other with a joyful and a ready will. Sealed by mutual faithfulness and hallowed above all by Christ's sacrament, this love remains steadfastly true in body and in mind, in bright days or dark" (Pastoral Const. on Church in Modern World, n. 49).

Speaking to newlyweds, Pope Pius XII said: "Matrimony is not, for you, a purely natural alliance, a merely human pact. It is a contract in which God has His place, which in truth is the first place. You were united before His altar, not only to lighten each other's burden during this life, but further still to collaborate with God Himself for the continuation of His creative, preservative and redemptive work. Receiving and blessing your promises, God at the same time conferred on you a special grace to make all the more easy the fulfillment of new and special duties."

Sex must be viewed in this light. Some people, however, have a puritanical idea of sex. Others think that sex *is* love. Some, as Pope Pius XII pointed out, "would allege that happiness in marriage is in direct proportion to the reciprocal enjoyment of conjugal relations." He goes on to add:

"It is not so: indeed, happiness in marriage is in direct proportion to the mutual respect of the partners, even in their intimate relations; not that they regard as immoral and refuse what nature offers and what the Creator has given, but because this respect, and the mutual esteem which it produces, is one of the strongest elements of a pure love, and for this reason all the more tender."

SEX IS AN EXPRESSION OF LOVE

Sex is not love. It is an expression of love that is good and holy, created by God, "who made man from the beginning male and female" (Mt. 19:4), and said to them, "Increase and multiply" (Gen. 1:28).

Sex is a privileged gift, which God intended to be used only in marriage, enabling husband and wife to bring the pure love they had for each other before marriage to a perfect completion in the sacrament of Matrimony. A couple should have a reverence for this gift of God and recognize that sex is intended to draw men and women to God through its proper use and not away from God through abuse.

In the *Pastoral Constitution on the Church in the Modern World*, Vatican II says:

"The sexual characteristics of man and the human faculty of reproduction wonderfully exceed the dispositions of lower forms of life. Hence the acts themselves which are proper to conjugal love and which are exercised in accord with genuine human dignity must be honored with great reverence" (n. 51).

The teachings of the Church on the proper use of sex in marriage have been clearly passed on by Pope Pius XII:

"The same Creator, who in His bounty and wisdom willed to make use of the work of man and woman, by uniting them in matrimony, for the preservation and propagation of the human race, has also decreed that in this function the parties should experience pleasure and happiness of body and spirit. Husband and wife, therefore, by seeking and enjoying this pleasure do no wrong whatever. They accept what the Creator has destined for them.

"Nevertheless, here also, husband and wife must know how to keep themselves within the limits of a just moderation. As with the pleasure of food and drink, so with the sexual, they must not abandon themselves without restraint to the impulses of the senses.... Nature has given, truly, the instinctive desire for pleasure and sanctions it in the lawful marriage, not as an end in itself, but rather for the service of life."

"Conjugal chastity is not a new or inhuman law," said Paul VI speaking to the world's couples and families in February, 1966, "it is the doctrine of honesty and of wisdom which the Church, illumined by God, has always taught, and which joins with an indissoluble bond the legitimate expressions of conjugal love and the service of God in the mission deriving from Him of transmitting life. It is the doctrine which has ennobled and sanctified Christian conjugal love, purifying it from the selfishness of the flesh and the selfishness of the spirit, from a superficial seeking of the transient realities of this world in preference to the gift of oneself for something which is eternal.

"It is the doctrine and the virtue which, throughout the centuries, has redeemed woman from the slavery of a duty suffered under force and with humiliation, and has quickened the sense of mutual respect and the reciprocal esteem of the partners. Let them realize what a moral strength is stimulated and what spiritual riches are nourished by the virtue of purity, of conjugal life faithfully observed according to God's law. The serenity, the peace, the greatness of the mind, the purity of the spirit! Let them understand particularly the inestimable value it has in preparing them for their task as educators! It is as true now as in the past and always. Children find in the life of their parents the most profound formation of fidelity to God, while the parents find in obedience to God the certainty of the grace they need for their task as Christian educators, so difficult today.

"Let them not be discouraged by the difficulties they may encounter, and let them not, because of this, abandon fidelity to the Church. Entrusting themselves to divine grace, which they will earnestly pray for, let them, rather than reduce the divine law to the measure of their own will, raise themselves to the height of the divine ideal, renewing each day, from the start, that path of theirs which has as its goal an eternity of life with God and as a prize here on earth a more profound and more beautifying love."

Conjugal chastity calls for real courage, sometimes even heroic courage, and trust in God's providence. But couples can always count on the grace of the great sacrament they have received. May they let no fashionable argument or disgraceful example lead them off the path of true, deep happiness in marriage!

INTERPRETERS OF GOD'S CREATIVE LOVE

Everyone looks for happiness, but when they get married, a man and a woman feel it especially close. They realize that from now on, they will be happy only if each gives happiness to the other. At every moment, in everything they do, and especially in their sexual relations, they will consider the other before self.

Theirs is a happiness precious in God's eyes. He was the first to talk of love, and He spoke of it better than anyone else. In fact, He placed it within us.

Theirs is a happiness destined to grow because it is not just for themselves but to give new life.

The desire for and love of the children God will send them must already be a part of the couple's love, of their plans, of their expectations.

If a couple were to decide before marriage that they would not allow their love to bear fruit, if they laid it down as a condition for their marriage that they would not have children, their marriage would be invalid. The wedding would be a deception, a farce.

In this regard, Pope Pius XI writes:

"Although matrimony is of its very nature of divine institution, the human will, too, enters into it and performs a most noble part. For each individual marriage, inasmuch as it is a conjugal union of a particular man and woman, arises only from the free consent of each of the spouses; and this free act of the will, by which each party hands over and accepts those rights proper to the state of marriage, is so necessary to constitute true marriage that it cannot be supplied by any human power. *This freedom, however, regards only the question whether the contracting parties really wish to enter upon matrimony or to marry this particular person; but the nature of matrimony is entirely independent of the free will of man, so that if one has once contracted matrimony he is thereby subject to its divinely made laws and its essential properties.* For the Angelic Doctor, writing on conjugal honor and on the offspring which is the fruit of marriage, says: 'These things are so contained in matrimony by the marriage pact itself that, if anything to the contrary were expressed in the consent which makes the marriage, it would not be a true marriage' " (St. Thomas Aquinas) (Christian Marriage, Dec. 31, 1930).

Just as everything is above-board between the partners, with no deception or sidestepping, so also the gift of life and the decision as to the number of the children will be the result of a choice made together, with awareness of their responsibility to God, to their conscience and to society—in accord always with the natural law and the teaching of the Church which interprets it in the light of the Gospel.

Obviously, self-control and at times sacrifice are called for, but husband and wife know well that any solution which is not upright—much worse, one which is utterly wrong such as artificial birth control or abortion—would be a profanation of married love. It would be a sign that something has gone wrong, a sign of a selfishness that dries up and extinguishes joy and affection between the couple.

"Parents should regard as their proper mission the task of transmitting human life and educating those to whom it has been transmitted. They should realize that they are thereby cooperators with the love of God the Creator, and are, so to speak, the interpreters of that love" (Church in the Modern World, n. 51).

WHO CAN REGULATE HUMA

"In the task of transmitting life, husbands and wives must conform their activity to the creative intention of God, expressed in the very nature of marriage and of its acts, and manifested by the constant teaching of the Church" (Of Human Life).

"All should be persuaded that human life and the task of transmitting it are not realities bound up with this world alone. Hence they cannot be measured or perceived only in terms of it, but always have a bearing on the eternal destiny of men" (Church in Modern World, n. 50).

In our times there is so much confusing talk about the regulation of births that it is essential before marriage to have clear ideas on this subject so as to prepare for a serene, happy future. For this reason, we shall look at the main parts of the encyclical *Humanae Vitae, Of Human Life*, and comments from authorities.

There are in general two methods of limiting the number of children. *The legitimate one is the use of rhythm, or periodic continence.* The other method involves the use of unnatural and therefore sinful means, such as *contraception, abortion, direct sterilization.*

Pius XI wrote: "Every attempt on the part of the married couple during the conjugal act or during the development of its natural consequences, to deprive it of its inherent power and to hinder the procreation of a new life is immoral. No 'indication' or need can change an action that is intrinsically immoral into an action that is moral and lawful." Pope Pius XII added: "This prescription holds good today and always, for it is not a mere precept of human right but the expression of a natural and divine law."

USE OF MEANS AGAINST PROCREATION

Pope Paul VI in his monumental encyclical *Humanae Vitae, Of Human Life,* says: "In the task of transmitting life, therefore, they (husbands and wives) are not free to proceed completely at will, as if they could determine in a wholly autonomous way the honest path to follow; but they must conform their activity to the creative intention of God, expressed in the very nature of marriage and of its acts, and manifested by the constant teaching of the Church.

"These acts, by which husband and wife are united in chaste intimacy, and by means of which human life is transmitted, are, as the council recalled, 'noble and worthy,' and they do not cease to be lawful if, for causes independent of the will of husband and wife, they are foreseen to be infecund, since they always remain ordained towards expressing and consolidating their union. In fact, as experience bears witness, not every conjugal act is followed by a new life. God has wisely disposed natural laws and rhythms of fecundity which, of themselves, cause a separation in the succession of births. Nonetheless the Church, calling men back to the observance of the norms of the natural law, as interpreted by their constant doctrine, teaches that *each and every marriage act (quilibet matrimonii usus) must remain open to the transmission of life....*

"We must once again declare that the direct interruption of the generative process already begun, and, above all, directly willed and procured abortion, even if for therapeutic reasons, are to be absolutely excluded as licit means for regulating birth.

"Equally to be excluded, as the teaching authority of the Church has frequently declared, is direct sterilization, whether perpetual or temporary, whether of the man or of the woman. Similarly excluded is every action which, *either in anticipation of the conjugal act, or in its accomplishment, or in the development of its natural consequences, proposes, whether as an end or as a means, to render procreation impossible.*"

When the Vicar of Christ was forced to speak out on this touchy issue, and spoke without compromise, his courageous and brilliant encyclical *Of Human Life* initiated varied reactions.

"THIS IS NOT OUR RULING—
IT IS THE LAW OF GOD"

"Our Encyclical 'Humanae vitae' has caused many reactions," soon wrote Pope Paul VI. "But as far as We recall, the Pope has never received so many spontaneous messages of gratitude and approval for the publication of a document as on this occasion. And these messages have poured in from every part of the world and from every class of people. We mention this to express Our cordial thanks to all those who have welcomed Our Encyclical Letter and assured Us of their support. May the Lord bless them.

"We know, of course, that there are many who have not appreciated Our teaching, and not a few have opposed it. We can, in a sense, understand their lack of comprehension and even their opposition. Our decision is not an easy one. It is not in line with a practice unfortunately widespread today which is regarded as convenient and, on the surface, helpful to family harmony and love.

"*Once again We would remind you that the ruling We have reaffirmed is not Our own. It originates from the very structure of life and love and human dignity, and is thus derived from the law of God.* It does not ignore the sociological and demographic conditions of our time. Contrary to what some seem to suppose, it is not in itself opposed to the rational limitation of births. It is not opposed to scientific research and therapeutic treatment, and still less to truly responsible parenthood. It does not even conflict with family peace and harmony. *It is just a moral law — demanding and austere — which is still binding today. It forbids the use of means which are directed against procreation and which thus degrade the purity of love and the purpose of married life.*

"*The duty of Our office and pastoral charity have led Us to speak out.* We therefore send a paternal greeting to all married couples and to all families who seek and find their moral strength and true happiness in the order willed by God. From Our heart We bless them and all of you, wishing you well in building a society based on the Christian way of life" (August, 1968).

CHRIST GAVE A GUIDE TO MEN

Regarding the encyclical, "Humanae Vitae," His Excellency, Most Rev. Robert F. Joyce, D.D., Bishop of Burlington, Vermont, wrote: "There are some clear principles involved in the current discussion on the recent encyclical of Pope Paul on the birth control issue.

"1. There is a teaching authority established in the world to guide men in their religious and moral spheres. It was established by Christ, who promised His guidance under the Holy Spirit for all times. *It is not human authority but divine.*

"2. It is not within the province or the power of this teaching authority, which is the Church, to change the teaching of Christ, to modify the moral law, or to set aside the natural law, even for the benefit of her heroic men and women facing problems in marriage.

"3. *What is right or wrong may not and cannot be decided by popular vote or by prevalent practice;* it is not determined by what people are doing or saying or favoring.

"4. *The Holy Father and the Church cannot base religious and moral principles upon what is popular, or what is temporarily expedient, or what is acceptable to the world, or what appears to be a comfortable, easy solution of problems.* Certainly the Pope and the Church know the difficulties people face and the temptations they meet, and have a profound sympathy for them; but like good parents with their children, they cannot condone wrong, or countenance what is destructive.

"5. Theologians study and speculate and express opinions, constantly differing among themselves, as do lawyers, doctors, engineers and all professionals. Their conclusions require and deserve serious study and consideration, but *they alone are not the Church, and it was not to them that Christ gave the commission to teach.*

"*Fundamental to all of this is faith, a lasting conviction that Christ gave a guide to men that they may have life.*"

Addressing their faithful, the Bishops of the United States asked a Christian response to the Encyclical "Humanae Vitae":

"The sacredness of Christian marriage makes it a special concern of the teaching mission of the Church. The recent encyclical letter of Pope Paul VI reflects this concern.

"The Holy Father, speaking as the supreme teacher of the Church, has reaffirmed the principles to be followed in forming the Christian consciences of married persons in carrying out their responsibilities.

"Recognizing his unique role in the Universal Church, we, the bishops of the Church in the United States, unite with him in calling upon our priests and people to receive with sincerity what he has taught, to study it carefully, and to form their consciences in its light.

"We are aware of the difficulties that this teaching lays upon so many of our conscientious married people. But we must face the reality that struggling to live out the will of God will often entail sacrifice.

"In confident trust in the firmness of their faith, in their loyalty to the Holy Father and to his office, and their reliance on divine help, we ask of them a true Christian response to this teaching" (July 31, 1968).

SUPREME TEACHER OF MORALS

"I have been asked to issue some guidelines of instruction for our priests and people, following the Holy Father's pronouncement on the question of birth control," wrote His Excellency, Most Rev. Robert E. Tracy, D.D., Bishop of Baton Rouge, Louisiana.

"Let me accordingly give to our clergy, religious and laity my position on the matter, as the local official teacher of faith and morals:

"1. The pronouncement of the Pope is clearly *'authoritative'* and, therefore, is to be accepted by everyone who claims the Catholic position as his own. The pronouncement gives not a Catholic position but THE Catholic position.

"2. The pronouncement is definite, unambiguous, and issued with the clear intent of aiding Catholics in forming their consciences. *It is an official pronouncement by the supreme interpreter and teacher of Christian morality.* This office and function of the Holy Father is incontestable in the light of the teaching of Vatican II in its document on 'The Church.' Certainly we can feel assured that in making his decision the Holy Father, in answer to his many earnest prayers, received that special guidance which Christ promised to the head of the Church in the person of St. Peter, the first Pope.

"3. *The term 'supreme teacher of the Church' is clearly intended to mean that the authoritative teaching of the Vicar of Christ may not be overturned or repudiated by any other teachers, even though they be the greatest theologians in the world.*

"4. Whether the authoritative teaching of the Pope be 'infallible' or not is obviously beside the point. Infallibility has always referred to a very small and well-defined area of papal pronouncements called 'ex cathedra.' Authoritativeness, on the other hand, is a common and widely recognized quality of papal pronouncements which, in view of Christ's mandate to Peter and his successors, makes these pronouncements *the best practical guide to be followed, here and now,* if one be disposed to avoid, in reasonable fashion, any rash action in solving religious, disciplinary, organizational, jurisdictional and moral problems.

"5. Even though this papal pronouncement on birth control be regarded as unfortunate by many — even by some highly placed theologians and officials — still we have this question: *What other authority in the world is there, under Catholic teaching, which can overrule an official pronouncement of the Pope?*

"6. *Emphasis on conscience is certainly in order. But that is exactly the point. Conscience is, after all, only one's intelligence reaching a decision following a reasonable effort to obtain all pertinent evidence, natural and supernatural (revealed) as to the morality of some act to be performed by one's self here and now. Now any such reasonable effort by a Catholic must necessarily include acceptance of the teaching that the Pope is the supreme teacher of morals.*

"7. In the present case of birth control, the Pope has carefully taken up, for five long years, every single argument that could possibly have been considered by any individual Catholic conscience; he has, moreover, consulted widely the opinion of a variety of experts in many fields. Indeed, he has established discourse and consultation more widely than any individuals or any group of theologians could possibly have done. His pronouncement is, therefore, not only authoritative, it is also based on a most careful investigation of the facts, as well as of all the various schools of theological thought of our day.

"8. *Some of us, undoubtedly, will be disappointed that the Pope did not take the following position: (1) That there is substantial theological opinion on both sides of the question of birth control; (2) That individual consciences, therefore, might simply have been allowed to follow, in honesty, any position which might seem to be solidly moral, at least in the view of the individual. But the fact is that the Pope did not accept this stance. He did give full consideration to the liberal position cited above. He studied it and consulted it for five years. Then deliberately, clearly and officially, he formally rejected it. And so there is no way now for any Catholic to continue to advance such a position in his personal life, his teaching, his preaching or in the exercise of his pastoral ministry, without formally repudiating the position of the Holy Father as the supreme teacher of morals in the Church. To make such a repudiation would, of course, involve a total departure from a fundamental and central teaching of the Catholic religion.*

"9. When the supreme teacher of morals in the Church states a moral conviction and teaching, the assumption is — and in this case it is clearly a fact — that all conditions and consequences bearing on the matter have been deeply and sympathetically considered. Yet no one — especially not a divinely appointed teacher — can tailor his teaching exclusively to considerations of sympathy for humanity nor to the difficulties he must face because of the possible unpopularity of his teaching. Nothing can be permitted to stand in the way of the truth, as he is given to see it. The Catholic world has been asking for guidance from its supreme teacher and so, after five years of intense consideration, that teacher has at length given the world his answer. And the Catholic world should simply accept it.

"10. Still, the adherence to moral standards and to truth is nearly always difficult, not only in marital matters, but in practically every area of human responsibility. *There are those who must make severe sacrifices in our world in order to remain honest, incorrupt, truthful, dutiful in office, responsible as teachers and reliable as parents and guardians of the young.* The responsible bishop and priest, particularly today, must be prepared to face many problems and difficulties. Nevertheless, all of us must admit that no prospect of sacrifice can liberate us from the truth as it is presented to us in the teaching of the Church. I am confident that our Catholic people in the end, therefore, will willingly accept the difficult teaching of God's Church as now presented to us by our Holy Father in God, Pope Paul VI" (August 2, 1968).

LESSER MEN WOULD BUCKLE

His Eminence John Cardinal Wright, commenting on the Encyclical *Humanae Vitae*, wrote:

"The pressures on Pope Paul to speak on contraception other than he did have been sustained and massive. They have been pressures of human respect, politics, prestigious opinion, emotional torment, threats that Church unity might be destroyed or ecumenical hopes dimmed, and, concentrating all these directly upon him, a virtually unanimous world press.

"These are pressures before which lesser men would buckle in their eagerness to enjoy popular favor, to preserve an image of modernity and to seem to lead into the better future while in fact merely following the dictates of the moment.

"In the face of such pressures, not all of them unworthy and some almost unendurable to the priestly, even the human spirit, the Holy Father's pronouncement must be seen by the just and generous as truly magnanimous and the Pope himself takes on heroic stature as a courageous teacher to our times, prophetic in the Old Testament sense, evangelical in the richest sense of the New.

"The sensitive among the devout may read his words with tears, tears of admiration for the valiant Vicar of Christ who must bear fearless witness to the truth and tears of compassion for all who must, with equal Christian valor, bear the burden of the human condition made objectively holy, even when existentially heartbreaking, by those demands of truth with which beauty and goodness must always be reconciled.

"Many Americans will see the situation in lighter perspective if they remember an incident, charged with like passionate controversy, which occurred on a lesser but important level of history not so many years ago. Given the acclaim some of the experts opposing the Holy Father presently command and the unpopularity he well knew his authoritative decision would provoke, world reaction to the Pope's bold, historic action recalls the excitement all over the United States the night of President Truman's plucky firing of Douglas MacArthur.

"The parallel is imperfect, of course; the Church is not literally an army and the setting forth of religious truth is not the same as the development of political or military tactic. However, the parallel is, in its way, instructive. The professionals have been fully consulted and patiently heard; the leader has finally spoken as only he could and should do.

"It now remains to be seen whether lesser spokesmen among the people of God have a sense of responsibility and order proportionate to that of the subordinate chieftains of the wisdom of the world. General MacArthur acted with great grace in response to his commander-in-chief and in accordance with the pledged word which constituted him in his proper place and dignity. One wonders whether we, in our various posts of competence and authority within the Church, will make good the assurances all parties gave from the beginning, gave and presumably meant, that our doctrinal opinions were speculative pending the pronouncement of the Pope; that our practical recommendations and disciplinary procedures were contingent upon the directives the Holy Father has now given without fear or ambiguity.

"Our conformity with this given word is the measure not only of our Catholic fidelity to the Pope but of our greatness, particularly, be it said pointedly, the greatness and the integrity of those specifically among us who teach or preach moral theology.

"In this connection, and in view of the position which certain journalistic and broadly theological circles have attempted to consign to the Pope in the controversy on contraception, it is well to note that the Holy Father is not and has not been a kind of referee between two schools of thought on the question. Some lecturers and writers, including a few within the household of the faith, have inaccurately and unjustly represented the so-called 'majority' and 'minority' groups within commissions counseling the Pope as mutually exclusive camps of opposition between which the Pope is maneuvred, by this construction of things, into acting as arbiter.

"The Pope is not a theological referee in a crisis of this kind. Rather mindful of apostolic responsibilities proper and special to him, aware of the requirements in conscience of his unique teaching office in the Church (as a matter of faith) and in the world (as a matter of history), *Pope Paul has heard all sides and now speaks not as a teacher among many teachers but as the supreme teacher,* under God, of the flock committed to him in Peter by Christ.

"*It is difficult to see how the Pope could have spoken on the central issue of direct artificial contraception other than he did.* The pretense that he would or should speak otherwise, especially any such pretense on the part of responsible theologians, has frequently been cruel to Pope Paul as a person and callous, often brutally so, to the conscientious, hard-pressed, decent Christians whom some writers have seemed intent on aligning into pressure groups for the embarrassment of their Father in Christ.

"The attack on the Holy Father will be manifold. It will be said that he has failed to conform to the spirit and insights of the world in which we are privileged to live; Sacred Scripture, from Isaia and Osee to St. Paul, will comfort him and confirm his conscience on this point. It will be said that history will judge harshly his effort to witness to truth and to serve humanity; a good defense can already be made against that facile argument, but, in any case, it is not the judgment of history that Paul must either fear or face.

"Most painful to him, and most shameful on the part of his critics, will be the suggestion that he has loftily branded millions of his flock, Catholics trapped in the mentality and the practice of contraception, as mortally sinful. He has, of course, done no such thing. Only God judges who, among the weak, the frustrated, the confused, the desperate, are sinners and who, in varying degrees and for a variety of reasons, may be diminished in their moral guilt.

"*What Pope Paul has done, what he had to do, is recall to a generation that does not like the word or fact that sin exists; that artificial contraception is objectively sinful; that those who impose it, foster it, counsel it, whether they be governments, experts, or—God forgive them!—spiritual directors, impose, foster and counsel objective sin—just as they would if they taught racism, hatred, fraud, injustice or impiety. The Holy Father has pointed out what is, in fact, sinful, not who is, alas, a sinner. This is what Christianity always requires us to do, nothing more and nothing less.* The Church denounces errors, not persons; it exposes false ideas rather than presumes to judge individuals or name names. The Pope has done his duty bravely and clearly, with prophetic service of human civilization and pastoral fidelity to divine faith. He has left to priests of truly pastoral spirit the patient but honest guidance of individual souls enmeshed in the problems which arise around the universal objective truth of the Church's moral teaching; this guidance confessors must give with tender sympathy for human weakness (it is also their own) and loving zeal for souls, but without violation of God's will and the teaching of His Church.

"How could Pope Paul have done or said other than he did? He has resisted the compulsions of the statistics, the economic determinism and the political absolutism of an age of computers and conformism destructive of the person. He has defended life and love against political controls and the selfishness ultimately destructive of both. With apostolic integrity he has braved the sneers of the cynical and the honest dissent of those who do not share his faith concerning the divine origins and eternal purposes of life and of love. Pope Paul, even as every Catholic Christian, must do everything humanly possible and divinely permitted to realize the hopes of humanity and to alleviate the woes of the world, beginning with the material poverty that inhibits the transmission of life and the cultural poverty that hampers the enjoyment of love. But he cannot call light darkness or darkness light, what is false true, what is evil good. This was forbidden him, in so many words, when he was consecrated a bishop, an authentic teacher in the Church, long before he acquired the awesome obligations which are his as Chief Shepherd of Christ's flock.

"God console, preserve, protect and strengthen him — and all the faithful!"

"GOD DID IT LONG AGO..."

His Excellency, Most Rev. Robert E. Lucey, S.T.D., Archbishop of San Antonio, Texas, wrote in regard to the encyclical on birth control — *Humanae Vitae:* "Some writers seemed to think that the Holy Father had enacted some new restrictive legislation in an arbitrary manner contrary to the advice of experts in the field of social progress. One alleged scientist proclaimed that the Holy Father's statement 're-affirmed a medieval theological concept which was a moral crime against humanity.' Actually the Pontiff's encyclical on artificial birth control is not ecclesiastical legislation. No law has been enacted by the papacy, by any sacred congregation, by the Senate of Bishops, by any human being. God did it long ago. Any Catholic who rejects the divine will in this matter must settle his account with God. He may be able to fool his friends, his pastor, even himself — but he can't get away from God."

SOME "WEIGHTY" OPINIONS

from the Patriarch of the Greek Orthodox Church

"...We are living close to You," His Holiness, Patriarch Athenagoras, assured Paul VI, "especially in these latter days when You have done well to publish the Encyclical *Humanae Vitae.* We are in full accord with You and We wish You every help of God for the continuation of Your mission in the world...."

In a statement released to the French Press Agency, the Ecumenical Patriarch said he approved *Humanae Vitae* without reservation. "I am in agreement with the Pope," said the Patriarch. "Paul VI could not have made a different pronouncement. He has the Gospel in his hands and wishes to safeguard the moral law, the interests and existence of the family and of nations. I am with the Pope, at his side, in all his acts, in his words and in programs...."

Another source, the Associated Press, reports a further statement of the Patriarch: "The Encyclical is consistent with the Bible. All the religious books, including the Bible and the Koran, favor the safeguarding of the family; in his Encyclical, the Pope followed the way of the Bible. It would not have been possible for us to expect he would have taken a different position."

from the French Catholic newspaper, "La Croix"

The Encyclical has been the subject of comment in every part of the world. In France, the Catholic Paper "La Croix" mentioned that the Encyclical was issued after a long period of expectation and reflection and added: "The longer the wait the more clearly it appeared that the greatest service that Paul VI could render to the Church and to the whole of humanity was to affirm anew in all its purity (bearing in mind recent scientific discoveries, social evolution and the growing appeal to responsible parenthood) the constant doctrine of the Church which gives to the problem its only true and profound solution.

"There will be misunderstandings. But the Church knows that, like her Divine Founder, she is a sign of contradiction. She is aware that, by upholding conjugal morality in its entirety, she is contributing to the building up of a civilization that is truly human. The long silence, the discussions which arose, the imprudences of certain theologians or moralists — all this may have given the impression in certain families that the Church was leaving the problem of birth control to the exclusive judgment of their own conscience. But the Second Vatican Council had already recalled that in this sector of life the morality of behavior does not depend only on sincerity of intention or on the evaluation of motives, but should be determined by objective criteria derived from the very nature of the person and of his acts."

from Methodist Bishop Corson of Philadelphia

His Excellency, Bishop Fred Pierce Corson, formerly president of the World Methodist Council and an official observer at the Second Vatican Council, congratulated Pope Paul VI for his "courage and dedication and...resistance to compromise" in the issuance of the papal encyclical on birth control.

The Methodist Bishop told the Pope in a telegram that he was "reminding the world of its religious, moral and doctrinal heritage."

"We are grateful," read the telegram, "for your courage and dedication and your resistance to compromise for the sake of fashion between spirit and matter. You are reminding the world of its religious, moral and doctrinal heritage. Bishop Fred P. Corson, Resident in Philadelphia."

from a Catholic doctor

"The Vicar of Christ has spoken. Pope Paul was guided by the same God who gave Moses the Ten Commandments, and it is mandatory on all Catholics, whether laymen or religious, to use their energies in guiding their families, their neighbors, and their communities to follow the laws of God, rather than engage in the hairsplitting activities that have been going on since the encyclical was made public.

"The misguided theory which has been expounded that where a doubt exists obedience is not necessary is the same thinking that is eating away at the moral code of our nation, and is slowly destroying the family as the foundation of a God-loving society." (G. G. Papola, M.D., at a meeting of the executive committee of the St. Francis of Assisi Catholic Physicians Guild in Philadelphia).

a message from Holland

"You have roused the Catholic People, Holy Father, not only with your magnificent 'Credo,' but also today with your clear reaffirmation of the doctrine of the Church.... You will receive the gratitude not only of many Dutch parents but also of their children who will realize that they owe their existence to the respect of the Church for the natural law."

from India

Mary Naidu, a Catholic member of Parliament in India, said to journalists that she esteemed very highly the encyclical "Humanae Vitae," and pointed out that it was in line with the teaching of the great spiritual leader of India, Mahatma Gandhi.

from Australia

Particularly significant were messages received from the laity: one was from three Catholic mothers in Australia. Several married couples expressed their thanks and promised a courageous loyalty. From a married couple in the town of Bath came the message: "Peter has spoken; the world does not approve but God approves."

from Norway

One of the first telegrams to arrive to thank the Holy Father was from a Protestant family in Norway which read, "Congratulations for the courageous Encyclical on human life against contraceptives—From fourteen happy children and their parents."

The "Whys" of Rhythm

Now, with regard to the *practice of rhythm, or periodic continence:* in itself, it is not sinful to limit marital relations to those times when conception is not so likely to occur, because if generation does not take place it is not due to acts excluding it but rather to the normal functioning of nature. It is understood, however, that the married couple must be ready to accept and to rear the child if conception should take place.

Paul VI states clearly: "If there are serious motives to space out births, which derive from the physical or psychological conditions of husband and wife, or from external conditions, the Church teaches that it is then licit to take into account the natural rhythms immanent in the generative functions, for the use of marriage in the infecund periods only, and in this way to regulate birth without offending the moral principles which have been recalled earlier" *Of Human Life).*

JUST MOTIVES

It should be stressed clearly at the outset that couples must not rush into a decision to use rhythm. They must be sure to have sufficient reasons for it, if it is to be morally justified. Married couples have a positive obligation to provide for the propagation of the human race, unless circum-

stances of a eugenic, medical, social or economic nature excuse them from fulfilling this obligation either temporarily or permanently.

Those who limit births for merely selfish motives often deeply regret it later on. In sharp contrast are the countless marriages built on sacrifice and unlimited trust in God's Providence.

In poverty and hard times, a young couple struggled together first through one difficulty then another. After the first child, which nearly caused the death of the young wife, the couple was advised: "no more children." How much they had hoped for a large happy family! Why not trust in God, who can do all things? Along came two other children. The last of them became a missionary sister working to bring souls to God. The other two are happily married.

After thirty years of marriage, serious illness came upon the scene. For one whole year the husband was in and out of hospitals and doctors' offices. Expensive medicines and treatments increased the bills as the wife struggled to maintain their home and the necessities of life. Their married daughters helped in whatever way they could. Their daughter in religion helped with her loving prayers and words of comfort.

Finally an operation reduced the husband to a critical condition. The love and support of his wife and family was what really kept him alive. Prayer after prayer stormed heaven in his behalf. As his feverish eyes darted around the bedside at his wife and three daughters (including the missionary who had just arrived from a great distance to be near him), he said, "Now everything will be easy. My girls are all here." He was not alone in his moment of trial. Nor had he ever been alone. His wife had remained beside him day and night. For six weeks she remained in the lobby of the hospital as he continued his fight to live. She would allow herself to leave for only a few hours at a time for fear that he might call. The outcome, fortunately, was a happy one. The man slowly recovered and was taken home. His two daughters who were nearby were a source of help as well as comfort. One stayed with him on her two days off work. The other, who did not work, stayed with him three days a week, and his wife stayed by him at night and over the weekends. His convalescence was long and tedious, but the entire family bore the burden with all the love and gratitude they could muster.

Time and again, older couples thank God for having given them the courage to raise a number of children who enriched their lives and are now their comfort.

WHY IS RHYTHM PERMISSIBLE?

As we have said, however, there can be times when, after mature reflection, a couple decides to practice rhythm. Why does the Church permit this practice?

"The Church is coherent with herself," explains the encyclical, *Of Human Life,* "when she considers recourse to the infecund periods to be licit, while at the same time condemning, as being always illicit, the use of means directly contrary to fecundation, even if such use is inspired by reasons which may appear honest and serious. In reality, there are essential differences between the two cases; in the former, the married couple make legitimate use of a natural disposition; in the latter, they impede the development of natural processes.

"It is true that, in the one and the other case, the married couple are concordant in the positive will of avoiding children for plausible reasons, seeking the certainty that offspring will not arrive; but it is also true that only in the former case are they able to renounce the use of marriage in the fecund periods when, for just motives, procreation is not desirable, while making use of it during infecund periods to manifest their affection and to safeguard their mutual fidelity. By so doing, they give proof of a truly and integrally honest love."

Before the practice of rhythm is begun the matter is to be submitted to the confessor's judgment. The advice of a competent physician should also be sought.

SELF-MASTERY

What must be done if, in certain delicate cases, the risk of motherhood involved even in the practice of rhythm must be avoided?

To this question there can be only one answer: *complete abstinence.* Is this impossible? Is such heroism unattainable? Definitely not.

In the words of Pius XII: "God does not oblige people to do the impossible. And He obliges married people to abstain, if their union cannot be fulfilled according to the laws of nature. Therefore, in this case abstinence is possible. It is wronging men and women of our times to deem them incapable of continuous heroism.

"The man who does not want to master himself is incapable of so doing. Also, he who believes he can do so, but counts merely on his own strength without sincerely and perseveringly seeking help from God, will be miserably disillusioned. As St. Augustine said, 'God does not command impossible things, but when He commands He warns us to do what can be done and to ask what cannot and gives us help so that we can.'"

Explains Pope Paul VI: "The teaching of the Church on the regulation of birth which promulgates the divine law will easily appear to many to be difficult or even impossible of actuation. And indeed, like all great beneficent realities, it demands serious engagement and much effort, individual, family and social effort. More than that, it would not be practicable without the help of God, who upholds and strengthens the good will of men. Yet, to anyone who reflects well, it cannot but be clear that such efforts ennoble man and are beneficial to the human community."

STERILIZATION

With regard to *sterilization,* in particular, which is being advocated by some as a "superior" method of birth control, Pius XI declared:

"Christian doctrine establishes, and the light of human reason makes it most clear, that private individuals have no power over the members of their bodies than that which pertains to their natural ends; and they are not free to destroy or mutilate their members, or in any other way render themselves unfit for their natural functions, except when no other provision can be made for the good of the whole body" (Christian Marriage).

Pius XII stated: "Direct sterilization, that which aims at making procreation impossible as both means and end, is a grave violation of the moral law, and therefore illicit. Direct sterilization, either permanent or temporary, of man or of woman, is illegal by virtue of the natural law from which, as you are aware, the Church has no power to dispense."

This doctrine is upheld by Pope Paul VI, as we have already noted:

"Equally to be excluded, as the teaching authority of the Church has frequently declared, is direct sterilization, whether perpetual or temporary, whether of the man or of the woman. Similarly excluded is every action which, either in anticipation of the conjugal act, or in its accomplishment or in the development of its natural consequences, proposes, whether as an end or as a means, to render procreation impossible."

Man's right over the members of his body does not give him the power to destroy or mutilate them so as to frustrate the purposes they were naturally designed by the Creator to fulfill.

However, as Pius XII also said, there are cases in which *indirect* sterilization is permissible when carried out for the good of the organism and not for the purpose of rendering procreation impossible. Paul VI reconfirms this by saying: "The Church on the contrary, does not at all consider illicit the use of those therapeutic means truly necessary to cure diseases of the organism, even if an impediment to procreation, which may be foreseen, should result therefrom, provided such impediment is not, for whatever motive, directly willed."

DEDICATION IS ITS OWN REWARD!

In conclusion, then, married people as everyone else, will find their joy and reward in performing the duties required by their state in life. This involves sacrifice, yes, but it is certain that when they pray for strength, they will receive the graces they need to accomplish their duty, no matter what the cost.

These words are reconfirmed by the Holy Father, Pope Paul, who said: "The new Pentecost of the Church for which the entire People of God has prayed intensely in recent years and which We hope the mercy of God will bestow on His Church, cannot be a time of greater moral leniency but must be one of greater commitment for all, including married Christians. 'Make your way in by the narrow gate...how small is the gate, how narrow the road that leads on to life'" (Mt. 7:13-14).

THE RIGHTS OF THE INNO

The unborn child is entitled to full protection from all direct attacks, even those of his parents, which might deny him the right to live.

Today the question of *abortion* has leaped into the public eye perhaps as never before. Because marriage and family are so closely bound up with the preservation of human life, any treatment of marriage should include a clear presentation of the evil of abortion.

"Abortion — the deliberate procuring of the miscarriage of a woman — is murder," stated Richard Cardinal Cushing, in opposing efforts to liberalize abortion laws. "A human life comes from God Himself and is inviolable. This has been recognized in every code of morality worthy of the name and in the civil laws of every civilized, organized society.

"The principle of the inviolability of human life which is at stake, admits of no compromise. Those who would destroy or weaken the laws of our several states condemning abortion are flying in the face of God's law and those moral standards which from time immemorial have been recognized by the conscience of the community. This is true regardless of the language in which the proponents of change may couch their efforts.

"It cannot be emphasized too strongly that the issue which is involved here is not a matter of mere public judgment. It goes far deeper than that, involving as it does, the commandment of God, 'You shall not kill.' It would be unthinkable that organized society in this land which has been so abundantly favored by almighty God would countenance the killing of an innocent unborn child, in direct violation of His commandment. It would be a tragic day indeed were society, in the name of progress or reform, to repeal or weaken those laws which have for their basis unchanging and unchangeable moral principles, and which find their roots and authority in the Author of the Universe.

"I, therefore, urge all persons of good will to unite in opposition to any attempt to tamper with the laws prohibiting abortions. Religion and morality have been and must continue to be the indispensable supports of good government."

SOCIETY MUST RETAIN ITS SANITY

In 1968 the bishop of New York State's eight Catholic dioceses issued an unprecedented pastoral letter calling on "all who sincerely wish society to retain its humanity while solving human problems" to oppose efforts to liberalize the state's eighty-year-old abortion laws:

DEARLY BELOVED IN CHRIST:

The purpose of this joint pastoral letter is to invite your most serious reflection on our position as Catholics regarding the right to life of every human being and our consequent opposition to abortion.

The right of innocent human beings to life is sacred and inviolable. It comes from God Himself. The Second Vatican Council in its *Pastoral Constitution on the Church in the Modern World* declared clearly the position of the Catholic Church regarding abortion:

"God," the council says, "has conferred on man the surpassing ministry of safeguarding life — a ministry which must be fulfilled in a manner worthy of man. Therefore from the moment of its conception, life must be guarded with the greatest care while abortion and infanticide are unspeakable crimes."

Since laws which allow abortion violate the unborn child's God-given right, we are opposed to any proposal to extend them. We urge you most strongly to do all in your power to prevent direct attacks on the lives of unborn children.

We are by no means blind to the sufferings of mothers and to the problems confronting some families. We shall always support every effort to alleviate human suffering and to solve personal and family problems, but we insist that any solution must respect the life of the innocent, defenseless, unborn child.

We earnestly hope that all who sincerely wish society to retain its humanity while solving human problems will join with us in defending the sanctity of the human right to life.

Devotedly yours in Christ,
The Archbishop and Bishops of the
Archdiocese of New York

FROM SPOKESMEN OF OTHER FAITHS

A Greek Orthodox Archbishop, a Protestant Minister and two Rabbis in New York added their weight to the opposition to the abortion reform bill:

"The liberalization of existing abortion laws would lead to a serious deterioration in American family life," they asserted.

"It must be stated for the public record that abortion is not strictly a sectarian issue, as its proponents would have us believe.

"Men of all creeds hold that life comes from God, the Creator, and belongs exclusively to Him. This exclusive ownership the Almighty has underlined in the commandment, 'You shall not kill.' To assume that abortion is not included in this prohibition is anti-religious.

"In this context, expressions such as 'invasion of privacy,' 'urgently needed modification of the law,' and 'unconstitutional' are irrelevant and misdirected, and simply confuse an issue that is as clear as decency.

"The public should not let high-powered, clever propaganda isolate certain segments of the religious community as the only opponents to the legalized destruction of the most helpless. And legislators would do well to recall to physicians their obligation to protect and preserve human life, not destroy it at its inception."

ARCHBISHOP IAKOVOS
Head of the Greek Orthodox Archdiocese of
North and South America
DR. NORMAN VINCENT PEALE
President of the Protestant Council, New York City
RABBI JULIUS G. NEUMANN
Congregation Zichron Moshe, Manhattan
RABBI JEHUDA MELBER
Briarwood Jewish Center, Queens

CATHOLIC LAYMEN SPEAK OUT

In New York, the State Catholic Welfare Committee told a legislation hearing:

"We urge that the unborn child, from the moment of conception, is entitled to the full protection of our social order from all direct attacks, even those of his parents, which might deny him the right to live."

The Catholic committee's secretary, Charles J. Tobin, said abortion is "a vital issue involving basic principles of public morality."

More than sixty Catholic lay organizations, plus Catholic spokesmen in law, medicine, social science and pyschiatry, attacked the proposal to permit abortions.

The legislature was warned that loosening of abortion laws in such nations as Sweden, Japan and Hungary has led to more, not fewer, illegal abortions and an increase in deaths of mothers.

In some states of the Union abortion has been legalized and in others legislation is pending to sanction it. More and more in the near future, Catholics will be faced with this dilemma. All the more reason, then, that they should know what the Church believes in this vital matter and the stand they must take. It is Catholic teaching that direct abortion is homicide, murder of the innocent, and therefore gravely sinful.

The following excerpt from a joint statement issued February 1, 1968, by Lawrence Cardinal Sheehan (Archbishop of Baltimore), Patrick Cardinal O'Boyle (Archbishop of Washington), and Rt. Rev. Paul J. Taggart (Administrator of the Wilmington diocese) sets forth clearly and unmistakably the Church's stand on this question:

"Only God, as the Author of human life, has absolute dominion over it. Civilized man has always recognized that society and the individual may exercise dominion over life only within narrow limits....

"Any law which imperils the right to life of innocent human persons is a social evil....

"Direct voluntary abortion of a non-viable human fetus is a grave evil. Modern microbiology has shown that there is no qualitative or essential difference between the fetus at the time of conception and the adult human person. To fix a point after conception for attributing the dignity of humanity to a human fetus is both arbitrary and without scientific foundation. Voluntary abortion is, therefore, an assault upon the life of an innocent human person not essentially different from any other willful destruction of an innocent human life.... It is our prayerful hope that all men of good will will reassess and re-emphasize their concern for the rights of all human beings and that the principle of reverence for human life, confirmed by logic and experience, will guide the minds of our legislators as they consider proposals for abortion law change."

In passing, it must be noted that the Second Vatican Council likewise condemned abortion. We read in the *Constitution on the Church in the Modern World:*

"Whatever is opposed to life itself, such as any type of murder, genocide, *abortion,* euthanasia or willful self-destruction, *whatever violates the integrity of the human person,* such as mutilation, torments inflicted on body or mind, attempts to coerce the will itself; *whatever insults human dignity,* such as subhuman living conditions, arbitrary imprisonment, deportation, slavery, prostitution, the selling of women and children; as well as disgraceful working conditions, where men are treated as mere tools for profit, rather than as free and responsible persons; all these things and others of their like are infamies indeed. They poison human society, but they do more harm to those who practice them than those who suffer from the injury. Moreover, they are a supreme dishonor to the Creator" (n. 27).

REVERENCE FOR HUMAN LIFE

The U.S. National Conference of Catholic Bishops stress reverence for human life: "We are now facing," they have written, "a determined effort to repeal totally all abortion laws — thereby resulting in abortion-on-demand.

"In a pastoral letter on *Human Life in Our Day* (November, 1968) we urged that 'society always be on the side of life,' that 'it never dictate, directly or indirectly, recourse to the prevention of life or to its destruction in any of its phases.' Our concern is heightened by the awareness that one of the dangers of a technological society is a tendency to adopt a limited view of man, to see man only for what he does or produces, and to overlook the source of man's dignity, the fact that he is made in the image of God, and that from the moment of his conception he is worthy of the full support of the human family of which he is a member.

"Consequently, we have frequently affirmed as our own the teaching of the Second Vatican Council, that 'whatever is opposed to life itself, such as any type of murder, genocide, abortion, euthanasia or willful self-destruction, whatever violates the integrity of the human person...all these things and others of their like are infamies indeed.' At the same time, we have emphasized that society has an obligation to safeguard the life of every person from the very beginning of that life, and to perfect a legal-political system that assures protection to the individual and the well-being of the community.

"We restate with strong conviction and growing concern our opposition to abortion. In so doing, we do not urge one ethical conviction as the sole basis of public policy, but we articulate the concerns that are also held by persons of other faiths and by specialists in the field of medicine, law and the social sciences.

"Fully aware of problem situations that may exist at times, such as illegitimacy, great emotional stress, possible disadvantage for the child after birth, we find no evidence that easy abortion laws will solve these problems. In fact, the termination of life in these particular situations violates our whole legal heritage, one that has always protected the right to life. Moreover, it allows for an extension of the principle that may well endanger the lives of persons who are senile, incurably ill, or unable fully to exercise all their faculties.

"We strongly urge a renewed positive attitude toward life and a new commitment to its protection and support. We affirm our social responsibility, together with all society, to bring encouragement, understanding and support to the victims of rape, to intensify our scientific investigation into the causes and cures of maternal disease and fetal abnormality, and to provide to all women adequate education and material sustenance to choose motherhood responsibly and freely in accord with our basic commitment to the sanctity of life.

"We are certain that respect for human dignity and the reverence for human life are such widely shared values in our society that the discussion by lawyers, doctors, ethicians, social scientists and all concerned citizens of ethical questions like abortion will lead to a deeper understanding of the eminent value and inviolability of human life" (April 17, 1969).

If after conception has taken place, the life of the mother is in danger, whose life should be suppressed—the child's or the mother's?

Neither may be killed so that the other can live. The doctor is bound to make every effort to save both, since both— mother and child—have an inherent right to life.

In fact, when conception takes place, God directly infuses a soul into that biological complexity. Consequently, a human being comes into existence in the maternal womb. That tiny defenseless body has the dignity of a person and

even if he is not born yet, he possesses the right to life. "Every human being," wrote Pope Pius XII, "even the infant in the mother's womb, has the right to life *immediately* from God, not from his parents or any human society or authority. There is therefore no man, no human authority, no medical 'indication' that can give the right to *direct*, deliberate suppression of an innocent human life at any stage. To do so is to commit a real murder."

The commandment, "You shall not kill," prohibits the suppression of a life *before, during* or *after* its birth.

Future husbands and wives, future fathers and mothers — every Christian, every human being today, in fact — must make a new commitment to the protection and support of life. In our day, when men are becoming so much more concerned about basic human rights — thank God! — we must not let the right to life of the unborn be trampled on.

In Brief...

1. *Can Catholic couples make their own decisions about the methods of birth control they will use, as long as their intentions are sincere?*

"When there is question of harmonizing conjugal love with the responsible transmission of life, the moral aspect of any procedure does not depend solely on sincere intentions or on an evaluation of motives. It must be determined by objective standards. These, based on the nature of the human person and his acts, preserve the full sense of mutual self-giving and human procreation in the context of true love. Such a goal cannot be achieved unless the virtue of conjugal chastity is sincerely practiced. Relying on these principles, *sons of the Church may not undertake methods of regulating procreation which are found blameworthy by the teaching authority of the Church in its unfolding of the divine law*" (Human Life in Our Day, American Bishops' Pastoral Letter).

2. *What great factor does Vatican Council II call to our attention regarding human life and the task of transmitting it?*

"Everyone should be persuaded that human life and the task of transmitting it are not realities bound up with this world alone. Hence they cannot be measured or perceived only in terms of it, but always have a bearing on the eternal destiny of men" (Constitution on Church in Modern World, n. 51).

3. *How must we understand the human love of a man and woman?*

Pope Paul speaks of conjugal love as "fully human," "a very special form of personal friendship," "faithful and exclusive until death," "a source of profound and lasting happiness." Such love, however, "is not exhausted by the communion between husband and wife, but is destined to continue, raising up new lives." There is an "objective moral order established by God," which requires that "each and every marriage act must remain open to the transmission of life" (Human Life in Our Day, American Bishops).

4. *How is the unitive and procreative meaning of marriage impaired?*

"Both conciliar and papal teaching, therefore, emphasize that the interrelation between the unitive meaning and the procreative meaning of marriage is impaired, even contradicted, when acts expressive of marital union are performed without love on the one hand and without openness to life on the other. Consistent with this, the encyclical sees the use of the periodic rhythms of nature, even though such use avoids rather than prevents conception, as morally imperfect if its motivation is primarily refusal of life rather than the human desire to share love within the spirituality of responsible parenthood" (Human Life in Our Day, American Bishops).

5. *Is the encyclical "Humanae Vitae" a negative proclamation?*

"The encyclical *Humanae Vitae* is not a negative proclamation, seeking only to prohibit artificial methods of contraception. In full awareness of population problems and family anxieties, *it is a defense of life and of love, a defense which challenges the prevailing spirit of the times.* Long range judgments may well find the moral insights of the encyclical prophetic and its world-view providential. There is already evidence that some peoples in economically underdeveloped areas may sense this more than those conditioned by the affluence of a privileged way of life" (Human Life in our Day, American Bishops).

6. *How do the American Bishops appraise the encyclical "Humanae Vitae"?*

"*The encyclical is a positive statement concerning the nature of conjugal love and responsible parenthood,* a statement which derives from a global vision of man, an integral view of marriage, and the first principles, at least, of a sound sexuality. *It is an obligatory statement,* consistent with moral convictions rooted in the traditions of Eastern and Western Christian faith; *it is an authoritative statement* solemnly interpreting imperatives which are divine rather than ecclesiastical in origin. It presents without ambiguity, doubt or hesitation the authentic teaching of the Church concerning the objective evil of that contraception which closes the marital act to the transmission of life, deliberately making it unfruitful. *United in collegial solidarity with the Successor of Peter, we proclaim this doctrine"* (Human Life in Our Day, American Bishops).

7. *Why is rhythm not directly opposed to the unitive and procreative purpose of marriage?*

"The encyclical reminds us that the use of the natural rhythms never involves a direct positive action against the possibility of life; artificial contraception always involves a direct positive action against the possibility of life. Correspondence with the natural rhythms remains essentially attuned to the unitive and procreative intent of the conjugal act even when the spouses are aware of the silence of nature to life" (Human Life in Our Day, American Bishops).

8. *Are there certain fundamental values which one can never directly oppose or contradict?*

"There are certain values which may not oblige us always to act on their behalf, but we are prohibited from ever acting directly against them by positive acts. Truth is such a value; life is surely another. It is one thing to say that an action against these values is inculpable, diminished in guilt, or subjectively defensible; it is quite another to defend it as objectively virtuous" (Human Life in Our Day, American Bishops).

9. *Is obedience to God's laws regarding sex in marriage easy?*

"No one pretends that responsible parenthood or even fidelity to the unitive love of marriage, as these are understood by the Church, is easy of attainment *without prayerful discipline.* Recourse to natural rhythms, for example, presents problems which the Holy Father has asked medical science to help solve. Chastity, as other virtues, is not mastered all at once or without sacrifice. It may involve failures and success, declines and growth, regressions in the midst of progress. A hierarchy of values that reflects a conformity to the example of Christ is neither easily achieved nor insured against loss. Moreover, Christians, however many their failures, will neither expect nor wish the Church to obscure the moral ideal in the light of which they press forward to perfection" (Human Life in Our Day, American Bishops).

10. *What if a couple falls into sin?*

"Let married couples, then, face up to the efforts needed, supported by the faith and hope which 'do not disappoint... because God's love has been poured into our hearts through the Holy Spirit, who has been given to us.' Let them implore divine assistance by persevering prayer; above all, let them draw from the source of grace and charity in the Eucharist. And if sin should still keep its hold over them, let them not be discouraged, but rather have recourse with humble perseverance to the mercy of God, which is poured forth in the sacrament of Penance. In this way they will be enabled to achieve the fullness of conjugal life" (Humanae Vitae, n. 24).

11. *How should couples pursue the ideal of chastity?*

"In the pursuit of the ideal of chastity, again as of every other virtue to which he is bound, the Christian must never lose heart; least of all, can he pretend that compromise is conquest. At all times, his mind and heart will echo St. Paul: 'Not that I have become perfect yet; I have not yet won, but I am still running, trying to capture the prize for which Christ Jesus captured me' (Phil. 3:12). In no case, does he suppose that the Church, in proposing such goals, teaches erroneously and needlessly burdens its members" (Human Life in Our Day, American Bishops).

12. *To whom does God entrust the power of calling human beings to life?*

Addressing newlyweds, Pope Pius XII said: "Beloved sons and daughters, you stand before the Creator as the appointed preparers of His ways, yet free and intimately responsible. It will depend on you also whether those 'innocent souls, who know nothing' (Wis. 12:18) shall come to the threshold of life, whom the embrace of infinite Love decompanions in the eternal happiness of heaven. But if, alas! they remain but magnificent images in God's mind when they could have been rays of Sun that illuminate every man who comes into this world, they will forever be but lights extinguished by men's cowardice and selfishness."

13. *Is a couple's power of transmitting life subject to any law or merely to their own free will?*

"While this power of transmitting life exalts you, it subjects you in its use to the law of God, whose severity towards those who culpably deviate from its high and true end must not surprise you. Let these be afraid, but you who are sincere and obedient Christians need not be afraid, for you have understood the close collaboration that exists between man and God in the transmission of life" (Pope Pius XII, allocution to newlyweds).

14. *Is there ever any justifiable reason for a couple to practice artificial birth control even for a short while?*
"No difficulty can arise that justifies the putting aside of the law of God which forbids all acts intrinsically evil. There is no possible circumstance in which husband and wife cannot, strengthened by the grace of God, fulfill faithfully their duties and preserve in wedlock their chastity unspotted. This truth of Christian Faith is expressed by the teaching of the Council of Trent. 'Let no one be so rash as to assert that which the Fathers of the Council have placed under ana-thema, namely that there are precepts of God impossible for the just to observe. God does not ask the impossible, but by His commands, instructs you to do what you are able, to pray for what you are not able that He may help you'" (Pope Pius XI, Christian Marriage).

15. *What did St. Augustine say about couples who would not stop at even the most extreme measures to remain childless?*
"Sometimes this lustful cruelty or cruel lust goes so far as to seek to procure a baneful sterility, and if this fails, the foetus conceived in the womb is in one way or another smoth-ered or evacuated, in the desire to destroy the offspring before it has life, or if it already lives in the womb, to kill it before it is born. If both man and woman are party to such practices they are not spouses at all; and if from the first they have car-ried on thus they have come together not for honest wedlock, but for impure gratification; if both are not party to these deeds, I make bold to say that either the one makes herself a mistress of the husband, or the other simply the paramour of his wife" (St. Augustine quoted from Pope Pius XI, Chris-tian Marriage).

16. *What is direct sterilization? Is it ever permitted?*
"It would be more than a mere lack of readiness in the ser-vice of life if an attack made by man were to concern not only a single act but should affect the organism itself to deprive it, by means of sterilization, of the faculty of procreating new life. Here, too, you have a clear rule in the Church's teaching to guide your behavior both interiorly and exteriorly. Direct

sterilization—that is, whose aim tends as a means or as an end at making procreation impossible—is a grave violation of the moral law and therefore unlawful" (Pope Pius XII, allocution to midwives).

GOD WAS THERE WHEN THEY MET

In every problem that arises, in every difficult decision, Christian couples must count on their love and God's.

As Christians, they are a part of the Family and the People of God. The Lord is always with them, but even more so in the essential moments of life by means of sacred acts which point to His presence, give His grace, lead into deeper intimacy with Him, and bring help and comfort.

With the first of these acts, Baptism, God accepts us into His family. Then with Confirmation, He gave us a more personal charge and the ability to carry it out. With Penance and Communion, He heals and feeds us.

Our participation in these interventions of God will become an ever more conscious one, and our response will be a commitment to live in accord with them.

Every married couple can say: "God was there when we met. He called us and led us to one another so that we would set out together on this road that is our vocation."

When they went to the altar, their "I do" was a sign of God's presence uplifting their love, sanctifying it, making it a giver of divine life. At that time, He gave them a new position in His family and the grace to occupy it worthily.

So it is that the marriage which consecrated their love was a sacrament, that is, an action of Christ present between them, a symbol of His union with the Church.

"Christ the Lord abundantly blessed this many-faceted love, welling up as it does from the fountain of divine love and structured as it is on the model of His union with His Church. For as God of old made Himself present to His people through a covenant of love and fidelity, so now the Savior of men and the Spouse of the Church comes into the lives of married Christians through the sacrament of matrimony. He abides with them thereafter so that just as He loved the Church and handed Himself over on her behalf, the spouses may love each other with perpetual fidelity through mutual self-bestowal....

"Christian spouses have a special sacrament by which they are fortified and receive a kind of consecration in the duties and dignity of their state. By virtue of this sacrament, as spouses fulfill their conjugal and family obligation, they are penetrated with the spirit of Christ, which suffuses their whole lives with faith, hope and charity. Thus they increasingly advance the perfection of their own personalities, as well as their mutual sanctification, and hence contribute jointly to the glory of God" (Church in the Modern World, n. 48).

WHAT PARENTHOOD CAN

Children in the home make all the difference in the world. Couples who once thought they needed only each other to be happy find in parenthood a joy previously unknown.

A certain young man was famed for his frequent pleasure¹ trips around the world. Popular and wealthy, he was able to satisfy his every desire and to go wherever his adventurous spirit dictated. Yet he was very much dissatisfied with life.

A friend had not seen him for two years when they met one day. Having heard of his marriage, he congratulated him.

"Do you know that I'm a father now!" he boomed exultantly. "Oh, it's great! I'm a changed man, I tell you." And he was. There was a glow, a heartiness, a radiant maturity about him that was completely new.

His friend walked away from that meeting thinking: that's what becoming a father can do, even to a restless rover like him.

ALL THE DIFFERENCE IN THE WORLD

Children in the home make all the difference in the world. Couples who once thought they needed only each other to be happy find in parenthood a joy previously unknown.

Recently, a young wife confided the reason for her newfound happiness in her marriage. When she had married the boy she had always loved, it seemed they would be perfectly happy, but it had soon become obvious that she was hiding a heavy heart. Now it was a real pleasure to see her genuine happiness as she sat in her living room, holding her one-year-old son on her lap and telling her story:

"We bought this rather large house two years ago," she began. "My husband has just finished painting it and it is quite attractive now.

"When we were married we rented a tiny apartment, but the landlady immediately warned us that she absolutely wouldn't permit children in her house. We lived there for a year, but my heart was broken. Finally, I broke down and

cried, begging my husband to listen to me. 'I want children,'
I sobbed.... As a result, we searched for and found this large
house.

"Now I am really happy," she concluded, patting her
son's chubby leg. "And so is my husband. If God wants to
send me even a dozen children, as He did my mother, we will
gladly accept them all."

Through the pen of the Apostle, St. Paul, the Holy Spirit
points out the greatness and joy of motherhood: God gives
the child to the mother but, together with the gift, He makes
her cooperate effectively at the opening of the flower, of
which He has deposited the germ in her womb, and this
cooperation becomes a way which leads her to her eternal
salvation: "Yet women will be saved by childbearing"
(1 Tim. 2:15).

Even though she was recovering from a very serious
automobile accident, one young woman cheerily greeted two
missionary sisters who came to visit her. "It happened six
months ago, Sisters," she explained. "It was New Year's Eve
and my husband and I were on our way home from the movies
when this car suddenly appeared — seemingly from nowhere —
and smashed into us. My husband was only slightly injured,
but as you can see" — here she indicated the walker she was
using to get around and then pointed to the long scars on her
face — "I didn't get off so lightly. Both my arms were broken
as well as my leg and most of my teeth were knocked out.
When I recover completely, it seems that one leg might be
shorter than the other. I guess God really let me have it, but
I know He only permits these things to happen to those who
can take them.

"Anyway, the worst thing that happened that night was
that I lost the baby. It would have been our first and was due
in a few months. I don't care about myself, Sisters...all I want
is to have another child. Please pray that this wonderful thing
will happen."

How well this young wife realized that children are a
blessing of God! Those who do not taste these joys find it
hard to believe that such tiny creatures can be a source of so
much intimate joy and delight.

THAT NEW BABY...

Father and *mother* are two sacred words which cause
good married couples to thrill with joy! Children are "human

bonds" which strengthen the affection of husband and wife. They perpetuate the parents' name and features; they inherit their good qualities—but unfortunately, their dark sides, too.

The young *mother-to-be* must keep herself serene and as happy as possible. Undue agitation and anxiety, violent anger, jealousy or inordinate fear and depression can have an adverse effect on the little one forming beneath her heart. It is very important that she eat properly, get enough sleep and exercise, and follow the doctor's directions.

The *father-in-waiting* is advised to be especially considerate of and reassuring to his wife at this time. He shouldn't be surprised if she becomes a little irritable or depressed at times for almost no reason at all. Calmness and understanding on his part will take care of the situation. A good book on pregnancy and childbirth will increase his understanding and clear up any doubts or fears he may have. Also he could go to the doctor at least once with his wife in order to hear a professional report of the situation and get some practical suggestions.

When the baby to be born is not the first child, wise parents will prepare the other children to receive the new family member. They can explain to them that the baby will be tiny and it will be some time before he or she will be walking, talking or playing. Children's interest can be aroused in watching baby grow and in teaching it new things. When mom and dad bring baby home from the hospital, it only takes a moment to stop and give a big hug to each of the other children. They would love to help hold the baby for a few minutes. When visitors come, the children can show them the new addition.

Perhaps the older children will demand more attention, go back to "babyish" ways, or complain about the extra work the new one gives. These are "tell-tale" signs of insecurity. A little temporary extra attention and affection, more time with mom and dad, a gift, a visit to the zoo—in these ways youngsters will be reassured of their parents' continued love. They will come to know that baby is not a rival but a friend, not on a higher standing, but on the same level—"he's (she's) one of us." Moreover, they will be disposed to share with him and to cooperate in the home by doing little chores while Mother takes care of him. One of the advantages, in fact, for children in a family of several is that they usually learn early to be considerate of others.

8. Looking

SACRIFICE THAT PAYS

Regarding the difficulties involved in raising a good-sized family, Pius XII said: "God visits large families with His Providence, to which the parents, especially poor ones, give an open testimony by placing in Providence their entire trust when human efforts are not sufficient. It is a trust well founded, and not in vain.... God does not deny the means to live to those He calls to life. Providence is a reality, a necessity of God the Creator."

One mother of six, awaiting her seventh child, said confidently, "God always provides. You know, it seems that every time we are going to have another baby my husband gets a raise in pay."

Moreover, children are not always children. They have a way of growing up and becoming a tremendous aid to the parents who sacrificed for them. God often shows His special favor for large families by calling their members to great glory. Did not the great Dominican saint, Catherine of Siena, the illustrious Jesuit, St. Robert Bellarmine, the humble St. Pius X, and the lovable Pope John XXIII — to cite a few examples — all come from large families?

Giving souls to God is the privilege of good Christian parents, and these souls are in turn their great reward. They are a living memorial to their parents, once the latter have departed from this life. They carry on the family name and bring honor to it by the witness of their own private and public lives. The circle of children surrounding generous parents today is a figure of the crown that will one day be theirs forever in heaven.

Along with the tremendous joys a family brings, no one will deny that there are sacrifices and worries — sacrifices of freedom to a great extent, sacrifice of sleep, of personal desires, worries over the health of the children, worries over finances. Real, constant self-sacrifice is indeed required of those who raise a good-sized family, particularly if the head of the home does not have a good, steady income. The budget is stretched and stretched; the funds go down, and payday seems far off.

To these problems is sometimes added the harassing comments of those who raise an eyebrow every time a new little one is on the way. What do mother and father do at times like this? Says one mother of ten: "We put our trust in God and go ahead! He always gets us through the roughest spots."

Through loving trust and faith, such parents grow spiritually. Their devotion to duty and their cooperation with the graces of the sacrament of Matrimony is a beautiful manifestation of their loyalty to our Lord and His Church.

"Christian married couples, then," says Pope Paul VI, "docile to her voice, must remember that their Christian vocation, which began at Baptism, is further specified and reinforced by the sacrament of Matrimony. By it husband and wife are strengthened and as it were consecrated for the faithful accomplishment of their proper duties, for the carrying out of their proper vocation even to perfection, and the Christian witness which is proper to them before the whole world. To them the Lord entrusts the task of making visible to men the holiness and sweetness of the law which unites the mutual love of husband and wife with their cooperation with the love of God, the author of human life."

SETTING THE EXAMPLE

Parents who make a wholehearted effort to lead exemplary lives experience the joy of seeing their "good points" imitated by their children. What greater human consolation could there be?

Once a little boy of five was left alone with his father at bedtime. After some maneuvering and a lot of fun, the father finally got the little fellow into his night clothes, and was about to lift him into bed when the child said, "But Daddy, I have to say my prayers." He knelt down beside his bed, joined his hands, raised his eyes to heaven and said his usual prayers. Then he paused, lifted his eyes to heaven again and prayed:

Dear God,
make me a great big good man,
like my daddy.

In a moment he was in bed, and in five minutes asleep. Then the father knelt by his son's bedside and prayed:

Dear Lord,
please make me a great big good man
like my boy thinks I am.

A father of two boys lit up a cigarette while talking with friends and then remarked rather shamefacedly: "I wouldn't be doing this if my boy were here."

Pressed for an explanation, he told how his seven-year-old had watched a TV presentation stressing the dangers of smoking and then, looking up at his six-footer Dad, had asked:

"Why don't you stop? You're going to get cancer and die."

Then, after a pause: "And you're the only one I've got!"

"So now," the man continued, "I'm trying my best to stop. So's my wife." And he added, "You know, it's amazing the things I do because of my kids!

"Boy, they do everything you do! I crossed my legs the other night and happened to glance over at my two boys: both had their legs crossed exactly like mine.

"I'm convinced that if I want my kids to grow up right, I've got to set the example. Take religion, for instance. I used to go to Mass pretty regularly, but that was about it. Now I go to confession and receive Communion every week! It's my oldest boy—I practically have to go. He's a worse nag than my wife!

"Seriously, though, being a father has done a lot for me. I realize more and more that I can't expect them to be what I'm not."

Words mean a lot to growing children, but there is no substitute for example. No one can spot inconsistencies between word and deed as well as a child can. For this reason, people spontaneously compliment the parents when they are impressed by a child's good behavior and thoughtfulness. Everyone realizes that for the most part, children owe what they are to their parents.

No wonder it is said that a child often brings out the best in his parents. It is really amazing what parenthood can do!

PROFILE OF
THE IDEAL WIFE AND

Sacrifice of personal comfort and convenience mean nothing to her when it is a question of making the ones she loves happy. That is a woman in love.

MORE PROFOUND IN LOVE

"In every great undertaking," a French thinker once wrote, "you will find *a woman* at the beginning and at the end."

Looking into the lives of great men, one is bound to find a woman—a wife, a mother, a sister, even a daughter—who was a source of inspiration and encouragement, comfort and support, and without whom the man may well have never become a success or at least so great a success.

Where does woman get such power? The answer lies in her heart. For a man, the heart is one half of his life; for the woman, it is the whole of it. "More superficial in all other things," explains De Bonald, "woman is more profound in love."

In the feminine personality the heart predominates. A striking proof of this is shown by her natural tenderness, sweetness, spirit of sacrifice and "intuition." See how a daughter loves her parents, how a wife devotes herself to her husband, even if he is aloof and indifferent; how a sister cares for her brothers even when they are contemptuous; how a mother tenderly guides her children in spite of their ingratitude. All this reveals woman's greatness of heart.

LOVE IN MARRIED LIFE

Married love is made up of a thousand very little things when it comes to actual daily life, and a woman in love shows her affections with little acts of tenderness, of kindness, of continuous daily patience, by anticipating desires, by consenting willingly, by showering little attentions on her husband. Life is made up of little things, as the sea is of raindrops, cloth of threads, mountains of atoms. A loving wife keeps herself appealing in appearance and delightful to talk with, to be with, to take places.

The wife of a certain very wealthy man was the outdoor type who could not have cared less what dress she put on and who had little interest in the so-called "feminine charms." Moreover, she was a reflective girl who loved to talk seriously on "deep subjects"—philosophy, theology, issues of world concern, spiritual topics....

Yet this very woman dressed beautifully, ran very successful parties, and made herself extremely attractive—all to please her husband, who wanted her that way. She was happy to do it for his sake, and so much did she love him that she never let him realize how much self-denial was involved in it for her. At the same time, she gradually led him to become more interested in things of the mind and spirit.

When a man sees his wife doing the things she knows will make him happy, when he sees her all wrapped up in making their home an appealing, inviting, happy place, he thinks more and more of her. And if she is anxious to hear how his day went—instead of bombarding him with one complaint after another about *her* day—he will gradually share more and more of his thoughts with her. His business life will never become a world of which she knows little or nothing. As they share every aspect of their lives, their love takes deeper and deeper root.

A wife who knows how to draw out her husband becomes his best confidante, and to her, rather than to business pals, he will turn for advice or—perhaps unconsciously—for that needed encouragement and word of sincere praise.

"GOING OVERBOARD?"

Yes, a man wants his wife to support and encourage him. As a man, characteristics of pride and ambition predominate in him, but at times he feels very insecure. The wife who emphasizes his good points (to him, to the children, to friends and relatives) and who speaks optimistically about the future bolsters his sometimes flagging spirits.

A man craves recognition and success. He thinks about planning, building. He wants to achieve, to count for something. When these desires are frustrated, he becomes depressed.

If he finds stimulation and satisfaction in his work, life looks bright; if not, then it seems as if everything is going wrong. The wife who understands this will learn how to encourage him, how to make him feel that he is the bravest and wisest man in the world. She will show a great interest in his work, his friends, his viewpoints. Let her never give him that "taken for granted" feeling and let her never tire of being patient, loyal and sympathetic.

Especially after a hard day's work does a man need to be greeted with affection and warmth—something hot to drink, possibly a bite to eat and "his paper, slippers and pipe." Going overboard? Oh, no. All these little attentions calm his ruffled spirits and make him mighty glad to be home. His wife's continual acceptance of him, her continual confidence in his abilities will give him that courage and determination he needs to succeed.

The loyal wife is satisfied with dad's paycheck and shows it by avoiding complaints and by "making things do." There are a thousand and one ways to economize and stretch those dollars. Her efforts to be contented with what he earns go a long way toward making him feel he is appreciated.

If a woman smothers her desire to pout, to quarrel, to show dissatisfaction, if she crushes selfishness, she will find her husband counting on her, respecting her, admiring her more and more.

"I knew I married a very affectionate, very attractive girl," one young husband said, "but I'm finding out that I also married *a very wonderful friend.*"

Is the woman the only one who has to keep the love alive? Doesn't the man have his part? He certainly does, but the wife is better fitted for the role. When things start to go wrong, she will be the first to notice it, and to do something about it. She will find ways to light the flames again.

Some wives, even when their husbands walk out on them, are so strong in spirit that they forgive, effect a reconciliation, and help build up a new bond of fidelity and love.

The more she loves, the more successful a woman is in keeping her husband's love. *We learn to love by loving.*

Woman sustains man with a noble spirit which is keenly sensitive to God, to virtue, to the beautiful and the good. She supports and helps him with her thousand and one sacrifices, little acts of unselfishness and devotion which often escape his eye.

America's own Blessed Elizabeth Seton, as a young wife and mother, showed marvelous qualities of generosity and perseverance in love when faced with the unexpected.

Elizabeth's father-in-law died suddenly. To her thirty-year-old husband William fell the responsibility of providing for the material and moral upbringing of his twelve brothers and sisters, in addition to looking after the family business which had become quite confused because of changing political conditions.

Undaunted by the overwhelming odds, Elizabeth made every effort to assist her husband in those troublesome times, and her ability in handling William's affairs was of great help to him. She spent many long hours not only during the day but also far into the night examining his papers, going over his account books and taking care of his correspondence. And yet, with the greatest thoughtfulness, she remained in the background, not making her help evident, and desiring only to relieve her husband's heavy burden. Her words were always of holy resignation—how to make sufferings count for heaven.

Elizabeth's heart was heavy at seeing her beloved husband suffering so intensely. This is revealed in several letters written during this time to her relatives:

"God knows that our happiness is now very limited," she wrote to her husband's aunt, "and He also knows that we don't expect anything better until time, which adjusts all things will adjust them for us also, or rather, will accustom us to this change which has stripped us of all that we held most dear. In these sad times I must sustain not only William's courage but also my own, especially since I am expecting the birth of my third child any day now."

Isn't it easy to see how good a wife and mother can be?

WHAT IF A WOMAN DOUBTS?

Jealousy is sadness and bitterness at the thought that one's husband or wife is unfaithful. What to do about jealousy? Usually the best policy is to believe everything good that one hears about the other and nothing bad. But there can be times when jealousy surfaces, despite good will.

If a woman has solid reasons to doubt her husband's faithfulness, what should she do? She should first make sure that this is not simply an impression that has grown without a real basis; she should make sure that she is not being fed false information by jealous acquaintances. Third parties with long tongues can be the ruin of a home: "A meddlesome tongue can drive virtuous women from their homes," says Sacred Scripture (Sirach 28:15).

When, instead, a woman's suspicions prove right, she should ask herself whether she may have brought on his infidelity herself by her lack of love, her neglect of her appearance and personal cleanliness, or her coldness and indifference.

Whatever the cause of a man's interest in other women, the remedy is always in prayer, in forgiving, and forgetting (at least in appearing to have forgotten the whole thing).

If, on the other hand, a woman accuses her husband bluntly of his infidelity, refuses to talk to him, or tries other means of punishing him, she will only make the situation worse. Let her rather be more affectionate, more pleasant to be with, so that her husband will not find the way closed to his return.

And if the husband is jealous? In this case, the woman's task is almost more demanding. She will have to try to eliminate everything that might look suspicious to him. Maybe she is not reserved enough with other men or not prudent about having visitors when her husband is out. Perhaps she is too cold with him so as to make him think that her heart is elsewhere.

Should she realize that she could do much better on these points, let her begin at once. A husband unconvinced by words may soon be convinced by actions.

If everything should prove useless, however, she can only accept this suffering patiently and live her married life with stronger faith, stronger hope, and stronger love.

FAMILY FIRST

Most modern mothers have participated in social activities from their youth. Many were job-holders before marriage. Thus they find homemaking and motherhood (especially when the children are very young) rather confining. An active, enthusiastic young mother may well be tempted to overdo her participation in religious, social and civic associations. While she does need the stimulation of some social activity outside the home, she must be careful lest she neglect her family by becoming involved in too many organizations. She must sacrifice her personal interests and desires in this regard for the sake of her husband and children, who rightly have first claim to her time and attention.

When the children are young, a mother wisely associates herself with those parish, school and community activities most closely related to her position in the family. Projects of wider scope can be supported later. Even though various organizations may be very worthwhile and mother may feel guilty in not participating, she realizes that the best contribution she can make to her parish, community and country is to be a loving and devoted wife and mother. The family is the basic unit of society; from it church, city and nation draw their future members. The better, the finer the home, the better and finer will those future citizens be.

that golden thread of the "divine"

It may sound old-fashioned, but it will always be true: A woman is as powerful as her prayer. Faith for her is something vibrant and living. In all the difficulties of life, it is natural for a woman to turn readily and confidently to God. And Christ, ever-generous, will never fail to reward her.

Mary, the gentle mother of Jesus, was the perfect model of womanhood. Her life shone with the most sublime and radiant examples of virtue and charm. Study and imitation of her is the woman's way to fulfillment.

Woman is more spiritual.

It is usually the wife who creates the spiritual atmosphere of the home. It is she who introduces the "fine touches," such as the saying of grace before and after meals, morning and evening prayers, particularly the rosary. She makes sure each member of the family attends church and receives the sacraments. If she cannot persuade her husband to accompany her, she tries to win him (and many times succeeds!) by her prayers and good example. This is really the best "psychology." She does not stoop to *nagging tactics.*

Keeping worthwhile Catholic literature available in the home is another way in which she can influence her family for the better. And in today's clamor, she is very careful to screen even Catholic periodicals to make sure they measure up to her home standards.

Even the man who is overly ambitious financially or politically or is addicted to some vice cannot fail to be moved in some way by the suggestions and examples of a good wife. Though he may have coarse habits, a man would experience keen disappointment on seeing his wife slide down to the same level.

One woman, the wife of a former alcoholic, relates, "Some of our friends used to ask me why I didn't go and get drunk with him just to show him what it looks like. But I just wouldn't lower myself. I prayed and prayed that he'd change and I tried to do as much charity as I could. Finally, he stopped drinking. How can I fully explain the joy I feel to see him kneeling beside me at Mass! And then, when I find him next to me at the communion rail—I have no words... only humble gratitude to my God."

"Let us go back to the origin of the world," writes the modern theologian, Father James Alberione. "When God created man, Holy Scripture says, He watched him and, touched by compassion at the sight of his solitude, said: — 'It is not good that the man is alone; I will make him a helper like himself' (Gen. 2:18). And God created woman to be man's helper. But to help him in what? In his works, in his sufferings? Yes, for suffering is most bitter when one suffers alone! To share his joys and his dreams of happiness? Yes, because one is less happy when joyful alone! And since man was not created for earth but for heaven, since God instilled into him heavenly hopes, sublime aspirations and desires, since the world is his place of exile whereas heaven is his homeland, the noblest mission of woman is to support man on this path, and lead him lovingly to a blessed eternity."

LOVE WILL OVERCOME HIM!

How does a woman succeed in keeping her husband interested for a lifetime?

Here is the secret of how to succeed: *win his heart.* Doubtless man has certain traits which give him accidental advantages over woman. Man, naturally proud, does not easily abdicate his position. At times, he even exaggerates his power, assuming attitudes which make him forget that woman is his companion. There may be, in the world, more husbands who tyrannize their wives than wives who dominate their husbands. But paradoxically the man who will not allow himself to be swayed by another's intelligence or commands will become as docile as a child in the hands of the woman who has won his heart. Such is the disposition of Divine Providence: that which woman cannot conquer with power, she conquers with love.

Sacrifice of personal comfort and convenience mean nothing to her when it is a question of making the ones she loves happy. That is a woman in love.

If something is bothering her, if she has something to suffer, a woman keeps it hidden, so as not to let it weigh on her husband and children. A strong woman can frequently put up with many things in silence and keep cheerfully giving of her love and service.

An immature woman, however, adds to family problems by complaining to friends, relatives and neighbors, by never admitting any personal mistake or fault. She will have to learn to overcome these habits, turn to God in prayer, and if she needs advice, to seek it from someone who can objectively judge the situation and be of real help.

How can a woman keep her husband at home during the long winter evenings, on holidays, or during his vacation?
Certainly not by nagging advice, and even less by peevishness and a quarrelsome disposition, but by making the home a place of affection, cleanliness and order; a place of respect and love of children, courtesy and tact in manners, cordiality, and, not least, well-prepared meals....

Husbands are driven from the home for many reasons. Among them we number neglect, laziness, disorder, filth, and personal untidiness in a woman. There are others: ill-humor and pride which breeds continual fault-finding and complaints. To round off the litany, we mention a mania for meticulous order and cleanliness and continual chattering about petty events.

A wife should frequently ask herself if her home is neat, attractive and comfortable. Does she encourage husband and children to enjoy it to the fullest? Does she welcome their friends into it?

If she has difficulties in housekeeping, she can even go to the trouble of taking an evening course in home economics, rely on recipe books and ask her mother for pointers.

The telephone is such a wonderful invention, but the lady of the house should not use it (abuse it rather) to the point of neglecting her housework. Even with the many modern appliances available, housework occupies much of a woman's time and energy. Yet when she sees how husband and children contentedly relax in the clean, "homey" atmosphere, her sacrifices to keep the house neat and orderly are amply rewarded.

Are the meals she serves nourishing and appetizingly prepared? Does she often make that extra effort to cook her husband's favorite dishes? Is the atmosphere at the table a happy, relaxed one (hint: no watching of TV during meals)? Are all the family members present at the main meal?

Although a woman should quiz herself on the above, she also must ask herself about her personal appearance.

Careful shopping with an eye to style, color and price will provide her with a moderate amount of attractive and modest clothing. She should ask herself if her husband is proud to be seen in public with her, even when she goes grocery shopping?

A quick switch into a fresh dress, a dab of lipstick, a touch of the comb to one's hair takes only a minute for the busy housewife before the man of the house arrives home. But how

much it means to him to be greeted by an attractive "Mrs." who shows by her neat and pleasant appearance that she considers him the number one love in her life.

Successful woman? Successful wife and mother? Certainly! She is the center and heart of her home, and her 'popularity' is of the truly lasting kind.

DAD- THE HEAD OF THI

The husband bears the responsibility for the whole family. He must be attentive to the needs of all, consider their feelings and stimulate their abilities so that they may develop into the persons God intended them to be. However, most decisions should be arrived at through mutual discussion by husband and wife.

A man wants to be the head of the family and he wants his wife to be the heart. As said before, this is the way the Creator planned it.

"However, this subjection (of the wife to her husband)," explains Pius XI, "does not deny or take away the liberty which fully belongs to the woman both in view of her dignity as a human person, and in view of her most noble office as wife and mother and companion. Nor does it bid her obey her husband's every request if not in harmony with right reason or with the dignity due a wife. Nor, finally, does it imply that the wife should be put on a level with those persons who in law are called minors.... But it forbids that exaggerated liberty which has no care for the good of the family; it forbids that in this body which is the family, the heart be separated from the head to the great detriment of the whole body and the proximate danger of ruin. For if the man is the head, the woman is the heart, and as he occupies the chief place in ruling, so she may and ought to claim for herself the chief place in love" (Christian Marriage).

Man and woman are both images of God and equal in dignity and rights as human beings. However, each sex has been endowed by God with different physical, intellectual and emotional characteristics in order that each may complement the other. The husband leads the family, provides strength, protection and material support. The wife warms the home with love and devotion, cares for the children and husband and elevates the whole family to high ideals in life.

If homes are to be happy ones, where harmony reigns and children turn out well, there is one requirement: *dad must be the recognized head.*

Yet the good Christian father is not a harsh despot, but rather a gentle ruler. At this point, we are reminded of a young man engaged to a wonderful girl who has an excellent job. He himself, however, is too lazy to find steady work. The little that he does earn is all spent on his beautiful car. It seems evident that he has no intention of accepting much responsibility in life, yet whenever he speaks of his forthcoming marriage, he boasts: "I'll be the boss in our house! I'll be the boss!" This definitely is *not* what is meant by the Christian concept of father as the head of the home!

First of all, husband and wife are equals in the Church's eyes. In all that regards the marriage, they have equal rights. The father's privileged position, his authority, is not to be used to serve his own interests and can never lawfully go beyond the purpose for which God ordained it—the good of the family. The *Dogmatic Constitution on the Church* explains: "Let the father of the family take the place of God among his children, and not only by his authority but by the upright example of his life also stand clearly in the first place."

Nature and training have made men more capable of making decisions for the good of all concerned, and less inclined to be influenced by personal considerations. Certainly this does not mean that men are better than women, but rather that a man and woman complement each other's qualities and each has a special though different contribution to make to the marriage. Thus, normally the husband should have the final say-so and be the one to decide the general course for the family to follow.

NOT AN HONORARY VICE-PRESIDENT

Samuel S. Leibowitz, senior judge of Brooklyn's highest criminal court, had some very thought-provoking things to say in an article entitled, *Nine Words Can Halt Delinquency.*

"It has seemed to me," he wrote, "that something down deep, simple and basic, must have disappeared from our way of life to have caused this revolt toward crime among our young people."

The nine-word principle which can do more for us with our juvenile delinquency problem is, according to Judge Leibowitz: *Put father back at the head of the family.*

A woman appreciates her husband's cooperation in raising and disciplining the children. In fact, as a father, this is part of his God-given responsibility. "Bringing home the bacon" is not enough. Serious consequences may result from the abdication by the husband and father of responsibilities that he should rightfully shoulder.

Ashly Montagu stressed this point: "When men abandon the upbringing of their children to their wives, a loss is suffered by everyone, but perhaps most of all by themselves.

For what they lose is the possibility of growth in themselves for being human which the stimulation of bringing up one's children gives." *Father becomes the head of the house by acting as one, not by being satisfied with the position of honorary vice-president.*

The husband bears the responsibility for the whole family. He must be attentive to the needs of all, consider their feelings and stimulate their abilities so that they may develop into the persons God intended them to be.

However, most decisions should be arrived at through mutual discussion by husband and wife. It is a foolish man who thinks he can learn nothing from his wife.

"Conscious that he is still a fallible human being, even though in the divine plan he is the head of the home," explains Cardinal Cushing, "the Christian father is a man of prayer, modeling his trust and confidence on the patron of all fathers, St. Joseph. Moreover, with prudence he realizes that 'two heads are wiser than one' and so he holds counsel frequently with his wife and seldom acts in important matters without her advice. Though his word is the final one, the Christian father does not delight in issuing commands—he rules rather by suggestion and by love. When the child appeals for permission the wise father does not say: 'Go ask your mother.' He says: 'I'll think it over' or 'Your mother and I will discuss it and reach a decision.' And later the father communicates the decision to the child.

"Mother and father exercise authority together when the request is not specifically in mother's sphere alone, or in the father's alone. The child cannot shuffle from one parent to another. Rather, he will develop an appreciation of what authority is and what role it plays in life. Neither should a child be able to play one parent against another, nor should one parent out-vote the other."

God gave the family its head—the father. If father relinquishes his position, neither he nor his wife nor his children will be happy. When, instead, he does not allow himself to become totally taken up with his work or activities outside the home, but rather shoulders his share of responsibility for the happiness of the home and the training of the children, it is easy for his family to look up to him as the true head of the family—worthy of the title.

DISCIPLINE — WHAT IT REALLY MEANS

A man has a hard job. He must convey the true meaning of discipline to his children. For many people, discipline means little more than punishment—such as standing in the corner, or a good old-fashioned spanking. But there is another side to it. Actually the word "discipline" itself is derived from the Latin verb "discere," signifying "to learn." The parent, therefore, who achieves true discipline does so by creating an atmosphere—both free and orderly—in which learning can be readily imparted and voluntarily assimilated.

If a man sees God's holy image in each of his children, then his exercise of authority will always be motivated by love. Furthermore, he will work hard to develop their latent abilities, highlight good qualities while not over-looking defects, help them to be self-reliant and resourceful, treat them always with the consideration that he expected when he was their age—while always having the courage to say "no" when he should.

Treating one's children as distinct individuals requires continual effort. Such considerations as these may help:

A reasonable amount of *order* is essential in raising a family, but "orderliness" should not be carried too far.

Children resist *over-protection*. They expect guidance but not domination, which stifles self-reliance and self-expression.

No one is in a better position than fathers and mothers to discover the qualities, abilities and inclinations that the Lord puts into each human being He sends into the world.

Children's need for privacy and quiet must be respected. They long for a chance to dream dreams, to unlock their imagination, to awaken their senses to the wonders of God's creation.

By satisfying their curiosity, letting them ask questions and attempting to solve difficult problems, a father can nour-ish their creative spark and launch them on a life-long voyage of discovery. Children will be thankful later in life if parents resist the temptation to hand them everything "on a platter." "Children need less protection and smothering love," one doctor said, "and more toughening and preparation for life."

Once youngsters are convinced that their ability is taken seriously, adults may be surprised to see how well they use their God-given energies. They can be taught to budget their study and leisure time...keep their rooms in order...help with younger brothers and sisters...do chores around the house... assist neighbors...find part time and summer jobs.

Fathers who develop the habit of regularly devoting a definite portion of their time to their families, even at per-sonal sacrifice, reap a twofold reward. They enrich the lives of their wives and children and make their own lives more complete.

THAT MAN WHO PAYS THE BILLS!

A child's love cannot be bought.

All the money and material goods which can be pro-vided mean far less to children than a sympathetic ear, sincere interest, words of encouragement and praise. A walking "money bag" is no substitute for a father. And what man wants his children to look upon him as merely "that man who pays the bills"?

One young woman recalls: "My father couldn't afford to buy us expensive gifts and toys, but he generously gave us something far more important—his time and his devotion. He built a swing, a slide and a sandbox for us and joined in our games. He was always ready to answer our questions and to point out some new fact or observation. He never failed to help us with our homework and showed a great interest in our projects, hobbies and activities.

"When I expressed interest in a bird-feeding station, he started to build one right away. One of us had to make a bug collection for biology class; he willingly helped to make an attractive display box and gave suggestions on how to improve the arrangement of the insects. He kept my teenage brother off the streets by fixing up the cellar as a recreation room, installing a billiard table and keeping him and his friends entertained. An approving smile, a reassuring hug, a word of praise from him meant more to me than all the money in the world."

A certain police chief, a stern-looking man, is quite another person when at play with his two adopted sons, ages ten and fourteen. To see him playing football with them is to see what a heart he has for those boys! And how they love to be with him!

DAD'S "CREDIT RATING"

Every man enjoys the satisfaction which comes from a job well done. When he has balanced his books, finding that all his accounts are straight and that he is making a profit, a warm feeling of contentment glows inside: his business is doing fine. But how about his business at home? How does he rate in the eyes of his wife and children?

There is no substitute for a good father! Few if any would disagree with this principle. In practice, however, it is not easy to live up to the unending requirements of being "a good father."

The more children see in his attitude and behavior a reflection of the Fatherhood of God, the more it helps them to lead purposeful, confident and creative lives.

The husband must be *strength, courage* and *leadership* to match his wife's tenderness, devotion and sympathy.

Strength must distinguish everything he does. An expert who has had considerable experience with fatherless boys maintains that such problems as "momism, weak family life, defections in the military, cheating in examinations, delinquency and crime, alcoholism and drug addiction, poor father images on TV, etc., etc." can be best overcome when the man of the house shows the fatherly strength which he can best provide.

As the breadwinner, a man must go out daily to his office, store or factory to earn a living for the family. Every morning he gets up, follows his schedule and makes it to work on time. Sometimes he feels like it; sometimes he does not. But his love and dedication give him the incentive to get out of bed and start a new day.

Naturally, he spends many hours on the job and may enjoy his work greatly. He must make sure, therefore, that he does not become so preoccupied with outside interests that he begins to take his wife and children for granted.

No matter how successful he may be on the job or in business ventures, life can be a failure if a man neglects to give his family the time and personal attention they need and deserve.

For example, he should never forget how to pay compliments. His wife will always enjoy—and very much so—being told that she is attractive, being noticed in a new dress, feeling that her husband is proud to be seen with her.

Especially at a certain point in her life, when the children are well on their way to adulthood, does a woman tend to feel insecure. Her youngsters are daily growing more independent, while she feels less needed. Likewise, her long preoccupation with child-rearing and household tasks has cut her off to some degree from wider contacts. She may feel that because of this, her husband seems to be living in a world apart from hers.

Affection, words of endearment, concern shown for her ideas, interests and problems will go a long way toward reassuring her of her husband's love. In fact, perhaps one of the most fundamental causes of a wife's insecurity in marriage is having doubts about her husband's love for her.

A man should realize this. When he was going with her, he made no secret of his admiration for her. After marriage, he should continue to show appreciation and consideration. He cannot say that by working to support his family he's done his share. Quite a bit of attention comes his way on the job and he receives much from his family. Doesn't his wife also deserve approval and recognition?

One of the secrets of having a contented wife is often giving her a "pat on the back." She doesn't hesitate to knock herself out for her husband because she loves him; she willingly bears and cares for the children; she'll make many sacrifices to economize and save. She never stops as long as there is work to be done. All she asks in return is love, respect and affection.

One young husband and father of three small children confided to a babysitter: "I'm glad you could come to watch the children for a few hours. You don't know what this means to my wife. She's not well and of course, the children keep her busy. This night out will do her a world of good."

A thoughtful husband takes his wife out. How she appreciates the refreshing change of scenery and a chance to spend a little time alone with her man.

If the wife objects to her husband's "night out with the boys," perhaps her resentment stems from the fact that it never occurs to him to take her out at all, or even better, an equal number of times. If he can't "afford" to take her out, then he can't afford *a night out with the boys* either.

MAN IN AN "APRON"

The model husband is helpful around the house, able and willing to make small repairs. He is even considerate enough to help his wife with the housework and shopping when she needs it. Here comes the protest: "But that's women's work!" Who said so? Marriage is a partnership, a sharing. The house and children are his responsibility as much as they are hers. A man can offer to dry the dishes once in a while, even though he'd rather watch that game on TV. Perhaps he could watch the children for an evening or on a Saturday afternoon while mother attends her club meeting or does some shopping.

WITH WOMEN—IT'S THE LITTLE THINGS THAT COUNT

Someone once said that it is a woman's world. The thoughtful husband who is building a life-time love doesn't mind going out of the way to make his partner happy. Here are some of the things he willingly does:

1. Unless it involves a long-distance call, he gives her a ring every day on the phone. Why not? It is so easy on his lunch hour and it takes but a minute or two.

2. He keeps his appearance neat around the house. If he wants to relax, he puts on sport clothes—casual, but still neat.

3. He brings her home a *surprise* now and then—even if small and inexpensive. It's the thought that counts.

4. He cooks dinner one night. True, all he does is open a few cans, or scramble some eggs. But his wife is thrilled. Then, best of all, he completes the job: He does the dishes afterwards and leaves the kitchen nice and clean.

5. He puts the children to bed one night. He makes her sit down in his easy chair and puts a good book or magazine in her hands.

6. When they relax for an evening of TV, he lets her pick the programs once in a while. (After all, to a woman there are more interesting things than a ball game or bowling championship.) Then, he sits down too, and joins her, cheerfully.

7. He keeps up those little courtesies practiced so carefully before marriage, things like opening and shutting doors for her, walking on the outside, rising when she enters a room. These mean so much!

8. He offers to dry dishes occasionally at night.

9. Once in a while, he takes her to dinner and then to a show, or dancing, or something she likes.

10. He shares stimulating conversations, talking about the office, about the children, about the good things they enjoy as a family, about mutual interests—yes, even about the world situation. He treats her like a well-versed adult, and not like a "know-nothing."

These are some sure ways to make a man number one in his wife's eyes. They are little things, true. Yet, blended together and mixed with effort and good will, they make for real marital happiness.

DIVORCE? SEPARATION?

10

If partners share each other's thoughts and concerns, if they work, pray and play together as a couple, right from the beginning of their marriage, their union will grow ever stronger. Yet, only God, with His law and His grace, can preserve husband and wife in mutual lasting love.

DIVORCE

No great good comes without sacrifice, they say. And marriage is no exception. Each partner must be ready to give in, to keep quiet sometimes, to take much with patience. "Christian spouses, however, are aware that they are never alone," says Pope Paul VI. "The Council reminds them that 'the Savior of men and the Spouse of the Church comes into the lives of married Christians through the sacrament of Matrimony. He abides with them thereafter so that just as he loved the Church and handed himself over on her behalf, the spouses may love each other with perpetual fidelity through mutual self-bestowal.'"

The immortal Augustine had words of high regard for his mother, St. Monica, for the way she kept peace in her home, despite her husband's infidelity, his complete lack of religious principles, and his hot temper. "My mother," affirms the saint, "made every effort to win him to God, preaching to him by her character, by which God made her beautiful to her husband, respected, loved and admired by him.

"She awaited God's mercy upon him, that he might grow chaste through faith in God. She knew, too, that a woman is wiser not to argue with a husband who is angry. Only when he had grown calm again would she give him an explanation of her actions, if he had been aroused to anger for no reason." We know further that she succeeded, by her exemplary life, in converting her husband to the Christian faith. Monica died a saint and the mother of a great saint. Hers, then, was a full, holy life, but because she *made* it so — by effort, prayer and patience.

how to prevent divorce

The Church suffers for those of her children who are unhappy with their lawful married partner, yet she can only exhort them to be patient and to pray for the strength and virtue they need.

On the part of those of her children who are contemplating marriage, the Church counsels — urges, in fact — due consideration and prayer in a matter so important. She advises them to seek the advice of their parents and confessor, since Holy Scripture says: "My son, do nothing without counsel, and you will not regret what you have done."

A girl of eighteen married the boy with whom she had been going steady since she was fifteen. Both the steady dating and the marriage itself were against her mother's advice. Yet she proudly went ahead with her plans, sure of her own decision. Now she is divorced. This action, too, was opposed by all her relatives. Yet she would not listen....

If only parents would think of their children, how many fewer divorces there would be! What havoc divorce works in the souls of youngsters! What agony in those hearts torn between parents; what suffering to have witnessed the bitter evidence of the hate existing between their father and mother!

If couples go into marriage well-prepared, they ought to know how to work on the personal faults threatening their happiness.

Knowledge of the problems of married life and its responsibilities, together with timely advice and guidance, would help keep many ill-matched couples from marrying and would prepare all couples in a practical fashion.

"Most unsuccessful marriages," says His Eminence, Richard Cardinal Cushing, "are doomed from the start, and I am convinced that the time to prevent divorce is before the marriage takes place, instead of afterwards. The most effective way to stop the growing prevalence of divorce would be to anticipate the conditions which make people seek divorce. That can be done only by an intelligent preparation for marriage on the part of those who intend to make marriage their vocation."

DRINKING AND DRUGS

Experts find that *drinking* rates the highest as a cause of marital failure.

An analysis of five thousand six hundred marriage failures showed *over-indulgence in drink* to be responsible for 29.8% of the cases. This percentage does not include those cases wherein excessive drinking developed only after certain maladjustments arose. In this 29.8% are included only those cases in which over-indulgence in liquor was the main source of the marriage failure.

Men are the chief offenders when it comes to drunken-ness. However, it is a well known fact that the drinking man is often accompanied by a nagging wife. Perhaps her constant scolding drove him to liquor or perhaps her vicious habit developed after he started hitting the bottle too often. In any case, nagging will not solve any problems; it only aggravates them.

The alcoholic husband or wife often loses the affection and respect of the sober partner and is usually not welcomed by friends, relatives and co-workers. A woman married to such a man is married to misery, as is a man wedded to an alcoholic wife.

How can children respect and receive good example from such a parent? And added to the social stigma are the other evils wrought by excessive use of alcohol.

Financial insecurity heads the list. One woman sighed, "I have to watch my pennies pretty carefully. My husband's a heavy drinker, so I'm never sure of having money. We're married for almost fifteen years and the children are about all that's holding us together." Another weary wife explained, "I have to work to help pay the bills. Over one third of my husband's pay goes into drink."

Other by-products of drinking are *irritableness, sullen-ness, harsh words* and even *brutal mistreatment of wife and children.*

Thirdly, excessive drinking can lead a person to *violate his vow of marital fidelity.* At bars and taverns he is brought into contact with doubtful characters of the opposite sex.

In dating and looking for a life partner, the only sensible advice is to avoid those who are heavy drinkers or are ob-viously on their way to becoming that. Sometimes a girl feels compassion and a yearning to "mother" a man who drinks but has some very appealing qualities when he is sober. She wants to be his "guiding star," his "angel," lifting him "out of the depths" by the power of her love....

It all sounds beautifully romantic, but the cold facts after such a marriage are generally quite different! When she tries in desperation to "convert" him, he is apt to snap, in both shame and anger: "You knew what you were getting into when you married me, so don't play the victim now!" And she wakes up to the plain fact that she has joined the sad ranks of women married to misery.

For the same reasons, *drug addicts* should be shunned when it comes to choosing a marriage partner. Real cures among addicts are quite rare. Those known to be on drugs should not even be dated, because drug addiction is catchy and seldom cured. Besides, even just a harmless date can sometimes spark the flame which leads to a passionate love, and then who can break up such a romance?

Staying away from certain places or persons may require a real sacrifice at first, but one will be reassured by the thought that he or she is giving up only a passing pleasure to insure true happiness for himself or herself and for the children God will send.

INFIDELITY

Another cause of marriage failure is *infidelity*.

Many people claim they believe in the sovereignty of God, in the last judgment, in heaven and hell, in each person's responsibility to God for his actions, but they live as if there were no God and no absolute moral code. Morals are put on the level with social customs. Many think that since divorce and remarriage are unfortunately becoming more and more socially acceptable, they can be permitted. Even some who feel a distaste for infidelity and avoid it themselves, condone the actions of others who are unfaithful. Flirtation of a married person with a third party is termed "just having a little fun." Even dates between a married man or woman and a third party are dismissed lightly by some and looked upon as a matter of personal option.

Vatican Council II in the *Constitution on the Church in the Modern World* states: "It (marriage) will never be profaned by adultery or divorce. Firmly established by the Lord, the unity of marriage will radiate from the equal personal dignity of wife and husband, a dignity acknowledged by mutual and total love."

Stable families can protect themselves from many temptations to infidelity by associating only with other stable families. It is true, of course, that husband and wife do not have the right to choose each other's friends. However, each does have the right and the obligation to warn the other about associations which, according to a reasonable judgment, are either dangerous or scandalous.

A wife's close association with divorcees may tempt her to become discontented with her own marriage or it may leave her with the wrong impression that "after all, there are some cases in which the Church should permit divorce and re-marriage."

A man who travels in the company of those who look upon marital infidelity as an adventure or as a clever game, rather than a grievous violation of the law of God and the rights of the partner, may be led to indiscretions which he would never dream of doing on his own.

Good families, therefore, should associate with one another and thus keep themselves as a group strong in their support of high Christian morals in family life.

winds of temptation

Where a third party is involved, the way to divorce is paved when one of the spouses *gives in* to temptation. All are disturbed by temptations against the sixth and ninth com-mandments. However, temptation is not sin. How many great saints—St. Benedict, St. Anthony, St. Catherine of Siena, to name just a few—had powerful temptations against chastity!

Yet, with the grace of God, those great "friends of God" triumphed and in the victory proved how true they were to their Lord. This can be everyone's story, just as it is the story of countless married men and women who are faithful to their marriage vows despite the powerful stimulations of a sexual nature so readily induced by advertisements, bill-boards, many immodest styles of clothing, some work situa-tions, and entertainment.

Chaste spouses are aware of temptation, but won't give it a second chance, a second glance. They realize only too well that temptation comes to them in the guise of a beautiful serpent. The offering is so attractive, but the resulting loss of God's grace and peace is as bitter and deadly as the venom of that snake.

Marriage counselors list two chief causes *of a wife's infidelity*. One is that domestic duties bore her and the responsibilities of child-rearing tie her down. The other is a lack of attention on the part of her husband.

Men, experts claim, *are unfaithful* because they are look-ing for adventure, sympathetic understanding of their prob-lems, or because their wives no longer make themselves or the home attractive and appealing.

The husband must make the life of his wife ever more interesting, caught up as she is in an endless round of monot-onous household duties; he must show her always more devotion and attention. Her challenge is to provide adventure for him. She must make herself even more attractive and appealing to him.

entertainment and dress

Still other causes of infidelity are *frivolous entertainments, reading and TV programs, and immodest dress.*

Some, particularly young couples, make the mistake of thinking that marriage renders everything permissible, *and they take the most imprudent liberties,* attending highly questionable amusement places. The husband may take his young wife to such spots, thinking to give her "a taste of life," and she may not have the good sense to recognize the evil of such actions and the dangers involved, or recognizing them, may protest only half-heartedly.

As for literature and TV shows, a steady diet of frivolous romances which make married life seem a purely sentimental adventure—enchanting, delightful, without cares or difficulties—can lead to trouble. A woman who compares such imaginary nonsense to her own married life, replete with financial worries and a thousand daily cares, may begin to think that she is missing real happiness. And how many dramas of infidelity have had no other origin but this?

Vatican Council II's Decree on the *Media of Social Communication* reminds us: "All who, of their own free choice, make use of these media of communications as readers, viewers or listeners have special obligations. For a proper choice demands *that they fully favor those presentations that are outstanding for their moral goodness, their knowledge and their artistic or technical merit.* They ought, however, to avoid those that may be a cause or occasion of spiritual harm to themselves or that can lead others into danger, or that hinder desirable presentations and promote those that are evil. To patronize such presentations in most instances would merely reward those who use these media only for profit."

Immodest dress on the part of the wife may well be the fault of her husband, who may encourage this practice to please her or to satisfy his own pride. But such imprudence exposes the woman and those with whom she comes in contact to innumerable dangers. The Christian wife must be modest in dress; she must have a clear idea of what is proper and must see to it that none of her clothes are offensive to the Lord.

diversity of opinion

Another cause of infidelity is *diversity of opinion and outlook*. During their engagement, the couple find each other's company absolutely delightful. They agree on everything. Yet, after their marriage, differences in viewpoint and values are not slow in appearing. Often a tragic hostility arises, and from this spring the so-called family battles. Trouble begins when both refuse to give in on unimportant matters, mere trifles, questions of personal taste or whim only.

The remedy? Each must deny himself and sacrifice his preferences in small matters as well as in more important ones. And each must be willing to bear with the other, to be understanding and sympathetic to the other's ideas. This requires sacrifice, but it pays off in happiness.

jealousy—we meet again!

And lastly, *infidelity can result from jealousy*—the poisoner of love. Jealousy is an unfounded suspicion of unfaithfulness on the part of husband or wife. The jealous person claims he ardently loves the other and thus demands unreasonably exclusive attention from his (or her) beloved. In reality the jealous partner has a very low estimation of his own worth and demands this constant exclusive devotion to cover up for his feelings of insecurity.

The remedy for jealousy is the constant remembrance of the fact that husband and wife are no longer separate, with individual interests, but that the two have become *one*. Thus, the honor and admiration which the one receives redounds to the other. When husband and wife view themselves in the light of this unity, each is happy to see the other excel in professional or social circles and make himself or herself well-liked by their mutual friends. Neither will be jealous or suspicious of the other. Nothing but warm affectionate harmony will reign between them.

If partners share each other's thoughts and concerns, if they work, pray and play together as a couple, right from the beginning of their marriage, their union will grow ever stronger. When children come, concern for their education and formation must draw mother and father even closer together. If husband and wife seek to minister to each other's needs, not only materially, but intellectually and emotionally, then neither one will be looking for fulfillment from an outside party.

Companionship is not something extra in marriage but a major goal and necessity of this union which should be the strongest and most intimate of human relationships, surpassing even that between parent and child.

One of the most important means of communication in marriage is, needless to say, talking. By sharing their opinions, ideas, and points of view, husband and wife get to know each other ever more intimately and grow ever closer together. They learn to be good listeners to each other; they learn to interest themselves in the other's feelings, experiences and attitudes.

The treasure of true matrimonial love enriches both husband and wife as together they achieve fulfillment.

"Let the spouses themselves," says Vatican II, "made to the image of the living God and enjoying the authentic dignity of persons, be joined to one another in equal affection, harmony of mind and the work of mutual sanctification. Thus, following Christ who is the principle of life, by the sacrifices and joys of their vocation and through their faithful love, married people can become witnesses of the mystery of love which the Lord revealed to the world by His dying and His rising up to life again" (Constitution on Church in Modern World, n. 52).

Christian love is not blind; it recognizes failings in the marriage partner, but it bears them with affectionate patience, fully conscious of personal faults. He who truly loves with a Christian love is always ready to see the good side, to interpret well, to excuse, to use kindness and avoid anything that might offend. Far from acting with superiority, he seeks his partner's advice and shows himself happy to receive it. Even should there be a storm in his heart, he knows that duty impels him, for his part, to be faithful to his marriage vows. Yet, only God, with His law and His grace, can preserve husband and wife in mutual lasting love.

Partners who have truly become *one* by dint of unselfish giving through the years grow ever more attached as time goes by.

"What will you do with yourself if you retire in a year or two?" a young woman asked her father. Then with a wink at her mother, she added, "You're not one to hang around night spots or go chasing after young women—"

At that her father threw back his head and had a good laugh.

"No!" he chuckled, "I'm not planning on that. I'm going to stick with Mom to the end!"

And as is perfectly obvious, this kind of unswerving devotion brings peace and contentment here on earth, and a great reward in heaven.

"A FEW JOYS AND MANY THORNS..."

Difference of temperament (in an extreme degree), *difficulties with in-laws, sexual maladjustment, mental illness* (this refers to cases in which one of the partners has been committed to an institution or has been diagnosed mentally sick by a psychiatrist), *very poor health* of one of the partners, *religious differences*, and *financial problems* are all reasons people give for seeking a divorce.

Those who seek divorce on petty grounds are obviously tragically selfish. But even those who have "good" reasons must place the welfare of others above personal happiness. They must shoulder their cross, as Christ did, out of love for others—for their children, for their partner, and for society as a whole.

Husbands and wives must be humble, so that when the failings and faults each hid during the courtship begin to make their appearance, they will know how to say, "I was wrong. I'm sorry." Oh, those two words, *I'm sorry*—how much peace and happiness they insure, and how much nobility of character they show!

In the course of a debate on whether divorce should be permitted, a young man spoke thus: "Having come to the end of my college career, I am fully convinced of the truth of my Faith. I believe in Jesus Christ. I esteem His sublime doctrine and I love it. As to the question of divorce, I can answer very briefly—I don't even need five minutes. I say that all those who are such strong advocates of divorce, in practice, when it comes to choosing a wife, do not choose a light-headed butterfly who believes in divorce, but just the opposite!"

In the same debate, a married woman from the audience declared, "I am a wife and mother and I say that what is argued in favor of divorce is inadmissible. Marriage must be indissoluble. Before we marry, we Christian women prepare ourselves for matrimony in a Christian manner, and we know that our marriage won't turn out perfect. That is impossible. But we are certain that God gives the necessary strength when, after the first days of roses, the thorns appear.

"For the Christian woman, even if by accident or sickness her husband is left an invalid or insane, he is always worthy of devoted love. We have our Faith to sustain us."

After her, a man rose to add, "Either we are Christians or we are not! If we are, we cannot treat the Gospel lightly. We married men want to raise morally healthy families; we want our children to have an ideal home."

Life is *a mission,* and it is in fulfilling our mission upon earth that we will find peace and happiness. And what is that mission? Simply to fulfill the will of God every day for a lifetime.

One day husbands and wives will be judged, not according to a civil law permitting divorce, but according to the holy law of God. So, if things seem unbearable, couples must pray, be strong, and remember that the heavenly reward is given only to those who strive for it and persevere to the end.

SEPARATION?

It may be asked: Is a "separation" the same thing as a "divorce"? Why does the Church at times permit a separation?

Pope Pius XI answers: "In certain circumstances, imperfect separation of the parties is allowed, the marriage bond not being severed. This separation, which the Church herself permits, and expressly mentions in her Canon Law in those canons which deal with the separation of the parties as to marital relationship and cohabitation, removes all the alleged inconveniences and dangers.

"It will be for the sacred law and, to some extent, also the civil law, in so far as civil matters are affected, to lay down the grounds, the conditions, the method and precautions to be taken in a case of this kind in order to safeguard the education of the children and the well-being of the family, and to remove all those evils which threaten the married persons, the children and the State" (Pope Pius XI, Christian Marriage).

when a separation?

The only thing, therefore, that the Church can do in cases which become unbearable, is to allow the partners of a valid marriage a *separation,* but without the right to marry again.

The chief cause of *perpetual separation* arises from adultery of one of the parties. There are other causes, however, which permit the injured party to seek *a separation:* criminal and shameful conduct, the education of the children in schism or heresy, grave peril of soul and body, etc. In this matter, the advice and direction of the pastor must be sought and followed.

A person may also lawfully sue for *a civil divorce* — provided he has no intention of remarrying — when the divorce is necessary to obtain certain civil rights *which cannot otherwise be obtained.* But before sueing for divorce, the person has to obtain the permission of the ecclesiastical authorities, and make a promise that he intends to procure its civil effects alone. Such a "divorce" has no effect whatsoever before God, and consequently the partners will remain married until death.

Parents hold the place of God for their children. They must, therefore, resolve to live in a spirit of unity — no matter what the difficulties of life. The example of their loving cooperation will remain with their children and be copied in their lives.

What They Ask About Divorce

1. Is married love meant to be permanent?

"There is rooted and living in the consciousness of both husband and wife a desire to belong totally one to the other, to remain faithful to each other in all the changes and chances of life, in the days of happiness and sadness, in health and sickness, in their first years' together as in their later years, without limit or conditions, until God wishes to call them to eternity. In this consciousness, in these intentions, human dignity is exalted, matrimony is exalted, nature is exalted which sees itself and its laws respected; the Church rejoices because in such a community of married life it sees shining forth the dawn of the family order established by God, and the summit of its divine restoration in Christ. When this is not verified, common life runs the risk of sliding into the pit of selfish desire, which seeks nothing but its own satisfaction, and thinks not of the personal dignity and honor of the partner" (Pope Pius XII, allocution to newlyweds).

2. If the will of a man and woman can form the marriage bond, can't that same will of theirs dissolve it?

The mere will of the contracting parties, though it can form the bond, cannot dissolve it. This is true not only for Christian marriage but for every valid marriage contracted on earth through the mutual consent of the partners.

"The 'yes' pronounced by your lips through the impulse of your will unites you by the marriage bond, and ties your wills together forever. Its effect is irrevocable: the sound, the sensible expression of your consent, passes away, but the consent, formally established, does not pass away; it is perpetual, because it is a consent established in the perpetuity of the bond, while a consent exchanged for only a certain period would not constitute between the parties true matrimony.

"The union of your 'yes' is indivisible; so much so that there is no true marriage without indissolubility, nor indissolubility without a true marriage" (Pope Pius XII, allocution to newlyweds).

3. *Can the Church dissolve a valid Catholic marriage? Can the Pope?*

"If the will of husband and wife cannot dissolve the bond of matrimony once it has been established, can the authority which is above them and established by Christ for the religious life of man do so? The bond of a Christian marriage is so strong that if it has reached full stability by the use of marriage rights, no power on earth, not even Our own as the Vicar of Christ, can dissolve it.

"It is true that we may recognize and declare that a marriage contracted as valid was in reality void, owing either to some diriment impediment, [1] or to an essential flaw in consent, or to a substantial defect in the form.

"We can also, in certain cases and for serious reasons, dissolve marriages which lack a sacramental character. [2]

"We can even dissolve the bonds of a Christian marriage, rescind the 'yes' pronounced before the altar, if there is a just and proportionate cause, when it has been established that the marriage has not been consummated by the conjugal act. But once that has taken place, that bond is beyond any human interference" (Pope Pius XII, allocution to newlyweds).

4. *Although the Church can never grant a divorce, she is able, if there is just cause, to declare a marriage null. Why is she so strict and hesitant in using this power?*

"As regards declarations of nullity of marriages, no one is unaware that the Church is hesitant and averse to granting them. Indeed, if the tranquillity, stability and safety of human

---

1. A diriment impediment makes an attempted marriage completely null and void — invalid. If a person attempts marriage without a dispensation, there is no marriage at all.

2. For example, there is what is known as the "Pauline privilege." In the First Epistle of St. Paul to the Corinthians (1 Cor. 7:12-15), we read: "If any brother has an unbelieving wife and she consents to live with him, let him not put her away. And if any woman has an unbelieving husband and he consents to live with her, let her not put away her husband.... But if the unbeliever departs, let him depart. For a brother or sister is not under bondage in such cases." Thus, the Pauline privilege applies in the following case: two unbaptized persons marry validly; one later receives Baptism; the other either departs or refuses to live with him (or her) without serious danger of grave sin against Faith or morals. The baptized party may have the marriage dissolved and be free to marry again.

commerce in general demands that contracts should not be declared null for every fickle reason, then all the more so must it be demanded of a contract of such importance as matrimony, whose firmness and stability are required by the common welfare of human society and by the private welfare of the wedded couples and of the children. Moreover, the dignity of the sacrament forbids that what is sacred and sacramental be easily exposed to the danger of profanation.

"Who is unaware then that human hearts are frequently and unfortunately inclined—for reasons of hardships of different kinds, or through disagreement and weariness with the other party, or to open the way to a union with another person sinfully loved—to study means to free themselves from the marriage union already contracted? For these reasons the ecclesiastical judge must not too easily be inclined to declare a marriage null, but rather to devote himself above all to see that what has been invalidly contracted be convalidated, especially when the circumstances of the case particularly suggest this course" (Pope Pius XII, allocution to the Tribunal of the Sacred Roman Rota).

5. *Supernaturally speaking (and isn't it only right to consider the supernatural, for man is more than just a well-bred animal), what helps a couple make their marriage work?*

"In the midst of difficulties, trials and inordinate desires which will perhaps be strewn along life's path, two souls inseparably joined will not find themselves alone or helpless. God's omnipotent grace, an essential fruit of the sacrament, will constantly be with them, to sustain them in the moments of weakness, to sweeten their sacrifice, to comfort and console them even in the hardest and longest trials."(Pope Pius XII, allocution to newlyweds).

6. *Is the indissolubility of marriage a burden or a guarantee?*

"Faced with this law of indissolubility, human passions, ever curbed by it and held back from the free satisfaction of their disordinate appetites, have sought in every way to cast off its yoke, wanting to see in it only a hard tyranny arbitrarily weighing down conscience with an unbearable load, with a slavery repugnant to the sacred rights of the human being. It is true that a bond may sometimes constitute a burden, a slavery, like the chains which fetter a prisoner. But it may also be a powerful aid and a sure guarantee, like the rope which binds the mountain climber to his companions in the ascent, or like the ligaments which unite the parts of the human body making it free and easy in its movements; and so is clearly the case with the indissoluble bond of marriage" (Pope Pius XII, allocution to newlyweds).

7. *Didn't God relax the law about the complete unity of marriage for His People of the Old Testament? Why can't there be dispensations from it now?*

"Conjugal faith, or honor, demands in the first place the complete unity of matrimony which the Creator Himself laid down in the beginning when He wished it to be not otherwise than between one man and one woman. And although afterwards this primeval law was relaxed to some extent by God, the Supreme Legislator, there is no doubt that the law of the Gospel fully restored that original and perfect unity, and abrogated all dispensations as the words of Christ and the constant teaching and action of the Church show plainly. With reason, therefore, does the sacred Council of Trent solemnly declare: 'Christ our Lord very clearly taught that in this bond two persons only are to be united and joined together when He said: "Therefore they are no longer two, but one flesh"' (Trent, session 24)." (Pope Pius XI, Christian Marriage).

8. *Aren't relations with a* **third** *party "less wrong" in our day and age?*

"They are destroying mutual fidelity who think that the ideas and morality of our present time concerning a certain harmful and false friendship with a third party can be countenanced, and who teach that a greater freedom of feeling and action in such external relations should be allowed to man and wife, particularly as many (so they consider) are possessed of an inborn sexual tendency which cannot be satisfied within the narrow limits of monogamous marriage.

"That rigid attitude which condemns all sensual affections and actions with a third party they imagine to be a narrowing of mind and heart, something obsolete, or an abject form of jealousy, and as a result they look upon whatever penal laws are passed by the State for the preserving of conjugal faith as void or to be abolished.

"Such unworthy and idle opinions are condemned by that noble instinct which is found in every chaste husband and wife, and even by the light of the testimony of nature alone,—a testimony that is sanctioned and confirmed by the command of God: 'You shall not commit adultery' (Exodus 20:14), and the words of Christ: 'Whosoever shall look on a woman to lust after her has already committed adultery with her in his heart' (Matt. 5:28).

"The force of this divine precept can never be weakened by any merely human custom, bad example or pretext of human progress, for just as it is the one and the same 'Jesus Christ, yesterday and today and the same forever' (Heb. 13:8), so it is the one and the same doctrine of Christ that abides and of which not one jot or tittle shall pass away till all is fulfilled (Matt. 5:18)" (Pope Pius XI, Christian Marriage).

9. *Should the Church relax her laws on divorce to meet current "trends"?*

"It is very true that in our times, in which contempt of and carelessness about religion have again given birth to the spirit of a new paganism that is pleasure-seeking and proud, there is manifested in not a few countries almost a mania for divorce, aiming at contracting and dissolving marriages with more facility and levity than is usual with contracts of leasing and hiring.

"But such a mania, thoughtless and inconsiderate, cannot be counted as a reason why ecclesiastical courts should desist from the norms and practice dictated and approved by sane judgment and a delicate conscience" (Pope Pius XII, allocution to the Tribunal of Sacred Roman Rota, October 3, 1941).

10. *What are the various arguments given for divorce?*

"Many and varied are the grounds put forward for divorce, some arising from the wickedness and the guilt of the persons concerned, others arising from the circumstances of the case. The former they describe as subjective, the latter as objective. In a word, they mean whatever might make married life hard or unpleasant. They strive to prove their contentions regarding these grounds for the divorce legislation they would bring about, by various arguments.

"Thus, in the first place, they maintain that it is for the good of either party that the one who is innocent should have the right to separate from the guilty, or that the guilty should be withdrawn from a union which is unpleasing to him and against his will. In the second place, they argue, the good of the child demands this, for he will be deprived of either a proper education or the natural fruits of it, and will too easily be affected by the discords and shortcomings of the parents, and drawn from the path of virtue. And thirdly the common good of society requires, they say, that these marriages should be completely dissolved, which are now incapable of producing their natural results, and that legal reparations should be allowed when crimes are to be feared as the result of the common habitation and intercourse of the parties.

"This last, they say, must be admitted to avoid the crimes being committed purposely with a view to obtaining the desired sentence of divorce for which the judge can legally loose the marriage bond, as also to prevent people from coming before the courts when it is obvious from the state of the case that they are lying and perjuring themselves, — all of which brings the court and the lawful authority into contempt.

"Hence the civil laws, in their opinion, have to be reformed to meet these new requirements, to suit the changes of the times and the changes in men's opinions, civil institutions and customs. Each of these reasons is considered by them as conclusive, so that all taken together offer a clear proof of the necessity of granting divorce in certain cases.

"Others, taking a step further, simply state that marriage, being a private contract, is, like other private contracts, to be left to the consent and good pleasure of both parties, and so can be dissolved for any reason whatsoever" (Pope Pius XI, Christian Marriage).

11. *Do these arguments in favor of divorce change the law of God?*

"Opposed to all these reckless opinions stands the unalterable law of God, fully confirmed by Christ, a law that can never be deprived of its force by the decrees of men, the ideas of a people or the will of any legislator: 'What God has joined together, let no man put asunder' (Matt. 19:6).

"And if any man, acting contrary to this law, shall have put asunder, his action is null and void, and the consequence remains, as Christ Himself has explicitly confirmed: 'Everyone who puts away his wife and marries another, commits adultery: and he who marries a woman who has been put away from her husband commits adultery' (Luke 16:18). Moreover, these words refer to every kind of marriage, even that which is natural and legitimate only; for, as has already been observed, that indissolubility, by which the loosening of the bond is once and for all removed from the whim of the parties and from every secular power, is a property of every true marriage.

"Let that solemn pronouncement of the Council of Trent, be recalled to mind in which, under the stigma of anathema, it condemned these errors: 'If anyone should say that on account of heresy or the hardships of co-habitation or a deliberate abuse of one party by the other the marriage tie may be loosened, let him be anathema.' And again: 'If anyone should say that the Church errs in having taught or in teaching that, according to the teaching of the Gospel and the apostles, the bond of marriage cannot be loosed because of the sin of adultery of either party; or that neither party, even though he be innocent, having given no cause for the sin of adultery, can contract another marriage during the lifetime of the other; and that he commits adultery who marries another after putting away his adulterous wife, and likewise that she commits adultery who puts away her husband and marries another: let him be anathema'" (Pope Pius XI, Christian Marriage).

12. *Does the approval of divorce laws degrade society?*

"Glance at modern society in the countries where divorce is rife and ask yourself: Has the world the clear knowledge and vision of how many times in those countries woman's dignity, outraged and offended, spurned and corrupted, is cast aside and almost buried in degradation and abandonment? How many secret tears have bathed certain thresholds, certain rooms; how many cries have resounded in certain meetings, along certain streets and byways, in certain corners and deserted haunts?

"No: the personal dignity of the husband and, even more that of the wife, has no better defense and safeguard than the indissolubility of matrimony. They are in grave error who believe that feminine culture and the dignity of women can be maintained, protected and elevated without basing it on the foundation of a matrimony one and indissoluble.

"When there is not fixed in the will the intention to guard perpetually and inviolably the marriage bond, there also grows enfeebled and decreases the consciousness of tranquillity and future safety for the father, mother and children, that sustaining feeling of unconditional reciprocal faith, that bond of strict and unchanging union (no matter what happens) in which one great and essential element of domestic happiness is rooted and nourished.

"Why, perhaps you will ask, do We extend such consequences to the children? Because they receive from their parents three great gifts: being, nourishment and upbringing, and they need a happy atmosphere for their healthy development. It is certain that a serene youth, a harmonious formation and education, are inconceivable without the undoubted fidelity of the parents. Do not the children nourish the bond of this married love? The rupture of this bond is cruelty towards them and contempt for their blood, a humiliating of their name, a division of their heart and a separation of brothers and home, a bitterness for their youthful happiness, and, what is worse still, moral scandal. How many are the wounds to the souls of millions of youths. In many cases, what sad and lamentable ruin! What implacable remorse is planted in souls! The Church and civil society place their hopes in spiritually upright, morally pure, happy and joyful men, who for the most part do not come from homes torn with discord and uncertain affection, but from those families wherein all is based on the fear of God and inviolate married fidelity" (Pope Pius XII, allocution to newlyweds).

13. *What effects has the practice of divorce had on our society?*

"Whoever wishes to know the reasons for the decay of contemporary morality and the poison which infects a great part of the human family will not be long in finding out that one of the most ill-omened and responsible sources is the legislation and practice of divorce.

"God's creations and laws always have a beneficial and powerful action; but when human neglect or malice intervenes and causes disorder and upheaval, an incalculable process of damage sets in, almost to the point where it seems that exasperated nature turns against man's work.

"Who can ever doubt or deny that the indissolubility of marriage is both a creation and law of God, a most valid support for the family, for the greatness of the nation?" (Pope Pius XII, allocution to newlyweds).

"Married couples and Christian parents," says the *Dogmatic Constitution on the Church,* "should follow their own path (to holiness) by faithful love. They should sustain one another in grace throughout the entire length of their lives. They should imbue their offspring, lovingly welcomed as God's gift, with Christian doctrine and the evangelical virtues. In this manner, they offer all men the example of unwearying and generous love!"

A LIFE FILLED WITH LOVE

Real love is unchanging, always youthful, untouched by the passing years. Indeed the years only serve to show each partner the real goodness, beauty and devotion of the other's heart, so that their mutual love is even more tender after fifty years, than in the first days of their married life.

Fidelity is the triumph of real love, the safeguard of affection in the home, the basis of a nation's greatness. Yet it is precisely this fidelity which is so fiercely attacked in our modern world.

Real love is unchanging, always youthful, untouched by the passing years. Indeed the years only serve to show each partner the real goodness, beauty and devotion of the other's heart, so that their mutual love is even more tender after fifty years, than in the first days of their married life. And in this love, husband and wife find strength to avoid all dangerous occasions.

WHAT THEY ASK ABOUT FAITHFUL LOVE

1. *Does mutual, total love demand virtue?*

"The constant fulfillment of the duties of this Christian vocation demands notable virtue. For this reason, strengthened by grace for holiness of life, the couple will painstakingly cultivate and pray for steadiness of love, largeheartedness and the spirit of sacrifice" (Church in Modern World, n. 49).

2. *Why does married life call for real heroism in many marriages?*

"In many cases a real heroism is required of Christian couples to respect the purposes of matrimony willed by God, or to resist the ardent and insistent stimulation of passions and the solicitations which lure a troubled heart to look elsewhere for that which it has not found in its lawful marriage, or does not believe itself to have found so fully as to repay all it had hoped.

"Again, if the bond of souls and mutual love is not to break or grow slack, the time may come when one must know how to forgive, to forget what is perhaps a serious discord, offense or wrong. How many intimate dramas lie hidden behind the veil of daily life! How many anxieties of the spirit in order that married couples may live together and remain constant in a Christian way to their own place of duty!" (Pope Pius XII, allocution to newlyweds).

3. *What attitudes should husbands and wives have regarding their mutual love?*

"This love is an eminently human one since it is directed from one person to another through an affection of the will; it involves the good of the whole person, and therefore can enrich the expressions of body and mind with a unique dignity, ennobling these expressions as special ingredients and signs of the friendship distinctive of marriage.

"Such love, merging the human with the divine, leads the spouses to a free and mutual gift of themselves, a gift providing itself by gentle affection and by deed; such love pervades the whole of their lives: indeed by its busy generosity it grows better and grows greater" (Church in Modern World, n. 49).

4. *Can wedding anniversary celebrations contribute toward the preservation of mutual fidelity?*

No less a personage than St. Francis de Sales, who was such an expert in the affairs of the human heart, says:

"I approve of the custom of making a feast on the anniversary day of one's wedding, provided it is not attended with preparations of worldly and sensual recreations. The husband and wife should confess and communicate on that day, and recommend to God, with a more than ordinary fervor, the happy progress of their marriage; renewing their good purposes to sanctify it still more and by mutual love and fidelity, and recovering breath as it were, in our Lord, in order to support with more ease the burdens of their calling."

5. *How can authentic married love be promoted?*

"Authentic conjugal love will be more highly prized, and wholesome public opinion created about it if Christian couples give outstanding witness to faithfulness and harmony in their love, and to their concern for educating their children; also, if they do their part in bringing about the needed cultural, psychological and social renewal on behalf of marriage and the family" (Church in Modern World, n. 49).

6. *What helps are couples given in their efforts to build a strong family life?*

"It devolves on priests duly trained about family matters to nurture the vocation of spouses by a variety of pastoral means, by preaching God's word, by liturgical worship, and by other spiritual aids to conjugal and family life; to sustain them sympathetically and patiently in difficulties, and to make them courageous through love, so that families which are truly illustrious can be formed.

"Various organizations, especially family associations, should try by their programs of instruction and action to strengthen young people and spouses themselves, particularly those recently wed, and to train them for family, social and apostolic life" (Church in Modern World, n. 52).

7. *What can married couples do to help protect family life on a national scale?*

"Christian married partners and the rest of the faithful should cooperate with men of good will to make sure that governments give due attention to the needs of the family regarding housing, the education of children, working conditions, social security, and taxes; and that in policy decisions affecting migrants their right to live together as a family should be safeguarded" (Decree on Apostolate of Laity, n. 11).

8. *In looking ahead to a happy marriage, how can young people prepare?*

"Especially in the heart of their own families, young people should be aptly and seasonably instructed in the dignity, duty and work of married love. Trained thus in the cultivation of chastity, they will be able at a suitable age to enter a marriage of their own after an honorable courtship" (Church in Modern World, n. 49).

MARRIED LOVE AND HOLINESS

"Although marriage is the common way of Christian life," said Paul VI, "and the path which the majority of God's sons are called to tread, it is not an easy one. It is rather a long path toward sanctification which, when it is guided by God's law and is imbued with love, nourishes itself on joy and on the daily sacrifices of what is apparently the most ordinary life."

For husband and wife marriage is the path to sainthood and to heaven. Taking care of the *round-the-clock* needs of their offspring is the way most parents fulfill the spiritual and corporal works of mercy. Housework, officework, or factorywork, done for God, can be noble and meritorious in His eyes. Children should not be considered an obstacle to union with God. Rather, it is through the children that parents grow closer to the Lord. Christ said that whatever we do for the least of His brethren we do for Him, and certainly children are included here.

A housewife of one parish was known for her "extraordinary" piety. It seemed that she was forever praying and she was present at every liturgical function. One day as she was making the stations (while two of her tots fought over candy under the front pew, and a third child howled disconsolately in a baby carriage outside the church door), she spotted the pastor, who had just dropped into church for a few minutes to make a visit. Immediately she made a beeline for the pew where he knelt.

"Father," she whispered anxiously, "do you think I should ask for a dispensation from my marriage vows and enter the convent?"

"Woman!" bellowed the priest, whose sharp eyes had not missed the antics of the three unattended children, "God made you a mother! That's your vocation! That is how He expects you to sanctify yourself! Now forget all about becoming a nun and go home and take care of your family!"

When a mother feeds and clothes her baby, she is serving Christ. When she watches over and teaches her growing youngsters, she is serving Christ. And when she guides and encourages her teen, she is also serving Christ. The mother and father who see Christ in their children and devote themselves unselfishly to their family cannot help but grow in love of God, which is, after all, genuine sanctity.

Because they must give example of what they teach, parents must ever strive to increase virtues in their own lives. The *Constitution on the Church in the Modern World* says: "The constant fulfillment of the duties of this Christian vocation demands notable virtue. For this reason, strengthened by grace for holiness of life, the couple will painstakingly cultivate and pray for steadiness of love, large-heartedness and the spirit of sacrifice."

Love of God cannot be divorced from love of neighbor. We show our love for God by being concerned about our neighbor's spiritual and temporal welfare, engaging in some type of *apostolic activity*. "For how can he who does not love his brother, whom he sees, love God, whom he does not see?" (1 John 4:20).

By their efforts and their interest in Christian values, husbands and wives participating in apostolic groups contribute toward making our society more truly Christian.

Not all individuals, due to personality or other circumstances, will be able to participate in organized groups, but they are always able to perform the apostolate of prayer, of good example, of kind words. In fact, they are obliged to do so, for Christ was not speaking only to the apostles when He commanded, "Go and teach all nations!"

Love is not static. One doesn't acquire love, and then keep it like a new piece of furniture....

Basically a saint is one who completely lives up to the divine command, "You shall love the Lord your God with your whole heart, and with your whole soul, and with your whole mind, and with your whole strength...you shall love your neighbor as yourself" (Mk. 12:30-31).

GOD LIVES WITH US

As a couple plans for their life together, much of their dreaming and planning centers around their future *home*.

Every detail involving the choice of the apartment or house and its furnishing bears the mark of their love and of their hopes.

All these arrangements can certainly contribute to their happiness, but only the living qualities within themselves can assure it.

The presence of God—with them and in them—felt so strongly when they received the sacrament of Matrimony, must continue to be felt in their home. As a witness to it, there will be a crucifix, a picture of the Blessed Mother, and more than that, their living faith, their fidelity to their Baptism, a Christian "atmosphere" which sanctifies work, relaxation, and all that goes into family living.

"The Christian family," says Vatican II, "which springs from marriage as a reflection of the loving covenant uniting Christ with the Church, and as a participation in that covenant, will manifest to all men Christ's living presence in the world.... This the family will do by the mutual love of the spouses, by their generous fruitfulness, their solidarity and faithfulness, and by the loving way in which all members of the family assist one another" (Church in the Modern World, n. 48).

Moreover, the Church where they were married or the new parish into which they move will be "their house," too, where they join others of the great family of God for active participation in the Sacred Liturgy. There, in the Mass, they meet Christ directly.

The Mass is the Lord's Supper—the sacrifice in which the Sacrifice of the Cross is perpetuated; a memorial of the death and resurrection of the Lord, who said "Do this in memory of me" (Lk. 22:19); and a sacred banquet in which, through the communion of the Body and Blood of the Lord, the People of God share the benefits of the Paschal Sacrifice.

As Christ (in the person of the priest) offers once again to the Eternal Father His perfect Sacrifice of Self which was accomplished on the cross, husband and wife join the offering of all their works, prayers and apostolic endeavors, their ordinary married and family life, their daily occupations, the hardships of life. All these become "spiritual sacrifices acceptable to God through Jesus Christ" (1 Pet. 2:5).

The Father shows His pleasure in receiving their offering of self in union with Christ by giving them in return His Son in Holy Communion. Communion is a vital part of the Mass, wherein Jesus Christ Himself, life and lifegiving in the Spirit, the source of all grace, strength and virtue, is received. How much courage He gives to parents who receive Him frequently! How much strength He gives them to accomplish faithfully their duties as husbands and wives, as fathers and mothers! And how deeply convinced of this many happily married couples are.

One Sunday during Mass, a young husband and wife, each holding a child, alternately fondled the little tots and turned the pages of their missals. At Communion time each arose, still holding a cooing and wiggling little one, and got into line to receive. No excuses of "too little time, too much to do because of the children" held them back from receiving their Savior and greatest Source of help in their married life.

From Mass and Communion parents bring Christ into their families and neighborhood, into their factory or office. Christ can become a vital part of society and culture through parents who are, so to speak, His hands and feet.

Another powerful means of living in Christ is the family rosary, said daily, if possible. Pope Pius XII urged:

"It is above all in the midst of the family that We desire that the custom of the holy rosary be spread everywhere, be religiously guarded and always further developed. Indeed, in vain is there sought a remedy to the vacillating destiny of civil life, if domestic society, the principle and foundation of human society, is not led back to the laws of the Gospel. We insist that to develop such an arduous duty, the Family Rosary is a more than efficacious means. What a pleasant sight and highly pleasing to God it is when, at eventide, the Christian house resounds to the frequent repetition of praise in honor of the great Queen of Heaven!"

The world will come to know *Christ's charity* through a couple's love of neighbor, *Christ's teaching* through their faith in His words, *Christ's examples* of virtue through their courageous imitation of Him in their own lives.

Part Three

CHOOSING ONE'S STATE IN LIFE

WHICH ONE FOR ME?

Since my life is a gift from God, what important points must I consider and weigh as the road of my future unravels before me?

This book has been dedicated to preparation for marriage, the road which the majority follow. These last two chapters, however, will deal with the other two roads in life: the single state and the religious state.

Choosing an ideal means choosing the mission one wants to perform. An ideal, a goal for which to strive fills a person with enthusiasm and offers a stimulating challenge.

There is a difference between a vocation or state in life and a career: one's state in life (there are three: the religious state, the single state lived in the world, and the married state) has to do with one's relationship to God and once entered, cannot be easily changed.

One's career, on the other hand, concerns the work one will take up, the occupation he or she will follow on this earth.

Since the decision as to his or her state in life affects the salvation of one's soul, the state in life should be chosen before the type of work is decided upon. God has given each person a vocation, that is, a calling to a particular state in life and in that particular state the person will find the most contentment and the most help from God in order to lead a fruitful life.

It is possible for a person to attain heaven by choosing a vocation which God had not intended for him or her, but the road is much more steep and much more difficult.... So, it is up to each one, with guidance and help, to find the state in life to which he or she has been called by God.

A young adult should consider each state in life with its particular requirements, then take into account his likes and dislikes, abilities and inclinations. He must see if he is drawn to a particular state and if he has the qualities demanded for success and contentment in that state.

The young person should seek the advice of his parents, teachers, counselors, and priest as to his choice of vocation. Above all, he should be encouraged to pray for God's help in making his selection and to base his final decision upon noble motives. The desire to dedicate one's life to the service of God, to spend one's talents in helping one's fellow man, to establish a home and family—all these are worthy aims. Choosing a state in life with a "what's-in-it-for-me" attitude will only lead to frustration and emptiness later on in life.

MARRIED LIFE

One who feels drawn to matrimony should ponder what it entails—love for the person he has freely chosen to spend his life with and love for the children God will send. And with true love automatically comes the opportunities—golden and frequent—for sacrifice and personal renunciation, and giving without counting the cost. This calls for maturity and genuine personality.

Marriage is holy because its success depends upon the practice of virtue. Raising a family requires many sacrifices on the part of husband and wife. *First and foremost is the practice of purity.* Young people must realize that if they do not guard their purity before marriage, they will hardly have the strength to remain faithful to their partner after marriage.

Regardless of what the movies say, true love is based on sacrifice. If they are willing to give up their desires, their pleasures for the sake of the other person, then they really love him or her. *The strength of love is measured by how much one is willing to give.*

Since marriage is ordained to the begetting and rearing of offspring, it is of utmost importance for one interested in the married state to have a great love for children. He or she must be willing to work hard — as a husband, to provide the necessities of life; as a wife, to care for the family.

Reflect deeply and ask yourself if you are willing to assume the *responsibilities* of marriage as described in this volume along with the happiness of a contented family circle.

SINGLE LIFE IN THE WORLD

The second type of vocation, the single state lived in the world, is misunderstood by many.

Some people have freely chosen to remain single even though marriage was possible for them. Stirred by the misery of many of their fellowmen, numerous unselfish men and women have given up marriage in order to devote themselves more completely to the service of humanity.

A certain number of persons decide to remain unmarried for selfish reasons: in order to avoid responsibility or in order to put all of their time and effort into becoming leaders in their profession. These are the single people who later in life will have reason to regret not getting married. They will realize how empty a career can be when followed for selfish motives and how unsatisfying it is to live for one's own pleasure.

it's all in the intention...

If one freely chooses to remain single in order to give all of his love and energies to God, then his state in life is even higher and holier than the very holy state of matrimony.

Mothers and fathers give God great honor and glory by rearing a truly Christian family and by their love of and fidelity to each other.

Yet, the person who chooses the single state for the love of God gives Him even greater honor and glory; it takes a truly generous, strong and pure soul voluntarily to give up the delights and consolations of marriage in order to devote himself or herself more completely to God.

perfect chastity — virtue of the strong

The foundation virtue of the single life in the world is chastity. One who feels called by God to live the single state in the world must practice perfect chastity: he or she must be determined to give up entirely and forever all pleasures of the flesh. Obviously, to practice perfect chastity for a lifetime amid the temptations of the world requires

great strength. Therefore, one who considers embracing the single state should most certainly seek the advice of his confessor before binding himself to lifelong chastity. However, one does not complete the requirements of the single state by just preserving perfect chastity; one must also struggle to acquire the other virtues of faith, charity, patience, humility, and so forth. It takes strength, courage and deep love of God to give up married life to embrace the single state. But what great good one can accomplish and what great joy and satisfaction will be achieved if one is willing to make the sacrifice!

Many married persons are hard-working lay apostles, but because of their numerous obligations as married people, they can give only a small part of their time to the apostolate. Single people, free from the cares of married life, do have the extra time to devote to this wonderful work.

SECULAR INSTITUTES *

There are associations of consecrated laymen and women who have dedicated themselves to follow Christ. These associations are called Secular Institutes. Their members bind themselves under vows, oaths, or promises to practice the evangelical counsels of poverty, chastity and obedience for the purpose of increasing their own personal sanctification while exercising an apostolate of love for Christ within the world.

Secular Institutes are characteristically different from religious communities. For example, they do not live a common life, in the sense of sharing a common roof and board. Their members stay in the world to work out their sanctification. Moreover, they do not take public vows as do religious.

This is a special vocation by which a person dedicates his life, through the evangelical counsels of chastity, poverty and obedience, to almighty God in his everyday work-a-day life.

THE LAY APOSTOLATE

Married or single, each and every Christian is an apostle. No matter what state of life a Christian chooses, he has the

---

* *Total Dedication for the Laity*, by Rev. Thomas P. McCarthy, CSV is a guidebook to Secular Institutes. It provides an outline of the aims and activities of more than twenty Secular Institutes. 104 pages; Cloth $2.00; Paper $1.00. Order from addresses at the end of this book.

duty of openly professing his faith and showing love to his neighbor. The *Decree on the Apostolate of the Laity* explains this point well, and lends new emphasis, new dimensions to the inner life. The following is a thought taken from the decree:

"The laity derives the right and duty to the apostolate from their union with Christ the head; incorporated into Christ's Mystical Body through Baptism and strengthened by the power of the Holy Spirit through Confirmation, they are assigned to the apostolate by the Lord Himself" (3).

"One of the lights which the Second Vatican Council sheds over the Church," said Pope Paul VI, "is *the vocation of every faithful member of the Church to spread the faith and Christian vitality,* to diffuse the inner fullness which his inclusion in the Mystical Body of Christ carries in itself. It is a vocation, furthermore, toward love of God's kingdom, toward a religious and moral witnessing which goes beyond himself and toward the need to communicate to others the treasure of truth and grace which he possesses — which, to use a term now become commonplace, we call *apostolate.*

"A layman, whatever his status, is called to this awareness, to this activity. There is need to emphasize this principle, because from it, to a great extent, comes the renewal and progress which the Council wanted to bring to the Church" (February 7, 1968).

Vatican II declared that "there are innumerable opportunities open to the laity for the exercise of their apostolate of evangelization and sanctification. *The very testimony of their Christian life and good works done in a supernatural spirit has the power to draw men to belief and to God;* for the Lord says, 'Even so let your light shine before men in order that they may see your good works and give glory to your Father who is in heaven' (Mt. 5:16)." (Decree on Apostolate of Laity, n. 6).

"for the charity of Christ impels us"

"However, an apostolate of this kind does not consist only in the witness of one's way of life; *a true apostle looks for opportunities to announce Christ by words addressed either to non-believers with a view of leading them to faith, or to the faithful with a view to instructing, strengthening and encouraging them to a more fervent life.* 'For the charity of Christ impels us' (2 Cor. 5:14). The words of the Apostle should echo in all hearts, 'Woe to me if I do not preach the Gospel' (1 Cor. 9:16)" (Decree on Apostolate of Laity, n. 6).

Following the same trend of thought and applying it to our own nation and day, the American bishops, in their first collective pastoral letter, remind us clearly of our identity with and responsibility to our neighbor:

"A Catholic becomes responsible when he realizes that his own dignity and destiny are bound up with the dignity and destiny of all men. A vocation to Catholic life is also a vocation of service to every member of the human family....

"A Catholic must be one who truly believes that as one of us suffers, all suffer, as one of us is healed, all are healed, when one of us is denied justice, all are threatened. Every Catholic conscience must respond in word and deed to the moral imperative addressed by Christ to nations as well as to men: 'Whatever you wish that men would do to you, do so to them' (Mt. 7:12).

"We seek Christ not only in the Scriptures but in the signs of the times; not only in the sacraments but in the hearts of men; not only in sacred Tradition but in all human cultures, in the human condition itself.

"Within recent years the Church has maintained the high level of its official teaching in encyclicals, in council, in synod, in papal addresses. She has borne dramatic witness to principle in *Mater et Magistra,* in *Pacem in Terris,* in the *Pastoral Constitution on the Church in the Modern World,* at the United Nations, and in *Progressio Populorum.* She has addressed herself to social justice, world peace, the political order, the underdeveloped nations. By all this, many were moved to put their hopes in her. *If Catholic performance does not match Catholic promise, then truly we shall have failed. If our deeds contradict our statements, then we shall have doubly sinned"* (The Church in Our Day).

THE RELIGIOUS LIFE

A religious vocation is a *special* call to *normal* people. Priests, brothers and sisters, believe it or not, were once young men and women, normal and active, often not exceptionally good but with a desire to become better. They had several characteristics: physical health, mental health, moral health, the desire to become a priest, brother or sister, the right intention, and also acceptance by the bishop or religious superior.

Proper physical health means a sound body. Proper mental health means at least average intelligence and emotional stability. To have sufficient moral health, one must be sincere, frank and generous. The right intention means that one wants to become a priest, a brother, or a sister for one or more of these reasons: the desire to love God with an undivided love, the desire to save souls, the desire to save one's own soul.

The bishop or religious superior cannot accept a person as a candidate for the priesthood, brotherhood, or sisterhood 1) if he or she is not of the right age; 2) if one is being forced against one's will to enter religious life; 3) or if parents will be unable to support themselves after he or she leaves home.

so nice...for someone else...

Have you ever wondered just how God calls those who follow Him? He invites souls to the religious life in different ways. Some boys and girls have felt from early youth the insistent desire to be a priest, a brother, or a sister. Other young people, however, feel toward the religious life a vague urging which comes and goes. To a certain number of others, the religious life is offered as a challenge, a way of life which seems to be very much against the person's natural leanings.

11. Looking Ahead to Marriage

In some cases God may desire a boy or girl to enter the religious state, but will not give the call to the person unless it is prayed for. One may have the proper physical, mental and moral health and yet not be sure if the religious life is for him or her. He or she should pray, then, to know God's will.

No matter how God makes a call to the religious life known, the person is eventually prompted to talk over his or her inclinations with a fervent priest or a dedicated religious superior. If the boy or girl meets all the requirements for entrance, then he or she can consider himself or herself called by God.

Many young people revere the religious vocation, but can hardly believe that they themselves are called. Knowing their own unexceptional qualities and human failings, they believe that *God must want someone better.* This is a mistake; if God is calling them, He will give them all the graces they need. Theirs is the duty of corresponding to the graces.

Religious life is a closer following of Christ and a choice of the *narrower way. Thus the Gospel is the supreme norm* of a religious. Even in our day genuine religious life calls for sacrifice, obedience, poverty, discipline, prayer, silence and seclusion. Pope Paul has often said that the youth of today are not afraid of sacrifice. Rather, what they do fear is the mediocre, and, at times, they even observe that not enough is asked of them, that there seems to be a kind of fear of confronting them with sacrifice....

one love — Jesus Christ

one burning desire — to give Him to souls

In choosing the virginal state and consecrating themselves completely to God, religious do not lose their capacity for paternal or maternal love. Rather, they enlarge and spiritualize it. Renouncing natural parenthood, they dedicate themselves to a moral, social and spiritual parenthood far nobler than the first.

Fathers and mothers cooperate with God in bringing *natural* life into this world. Priests, brothers and sisters cooperate with God in bringing *supernatural* life to souls.

The priest is actually another Christ: through the lips, hands and voice of the priest, our Lord still prays, blesses and forgives sins just as surely as He did during His life on earth. Jesus still offers Himself up to God the Father in satisfaction for our sins; He does this through His priest who in the holy sacrifice of the Mass offers to God the Body and Blood of Christ under the appearances of bread and wine. Since the sufferings of our Savior, which have an infinite value, are renewed in an unbloody manner during the Mass, every time a priest says Mass, graces are poured down upon the world. The parish priest, like the Divine Master, is a spiritual father who sacrifices himself willingly for the sake of the people of God.

Fervent brothers and sisters in religious life by their prayers, works and sacrifices obtain from God many graces for souls which help them to gain eternal life. Furthermore, brothers and sisters work among the poor and sick, closely and sympathetically united to them in their sufferings and problems, as mothers and fathers in spirit to the people they serve.

Because the priests, brothers and sisters who make of their vocation the close "following of Christ" and live their religious consecration in humble dedication and perfect chastity do not give themselves to just one man or woman, communicating natural life to a limited number of souls, they can give themselves to *all men and women* and through their fidelity to the Gospel and Christ's Vicar can draw supernatural life down upon countless numbers of souls.

Fortified by the vows of poverty, chastity and obedience, the religious dares to walk in the very footsteps of the Master. Dedicated to a specific apostolate in the Church, he seeks to direct souls to Jesus Christ in the tabernacle and to guide them to an intense interior life responsive to the insistent demands of our age for authentic Christian witness.

Religious are called to real heroism. They are asked to ascend from faith to trust, from trust to love, from love to contemplation, from contemplation to union, from union to heroism—heroism in virtue, in the practice of vows, in prayer, in silence, in total donation of self....

Therein lies the worth and dignity of the religious life. It was founded by Christ Himself, who said to the Gospel's rich young man: "If you want to be perfect, go, sell what you have and give to the poor, and come follow me" (Mt. 19:21).

"the great exchange"

Some well-meaning people believe that such a life of self-surrender is sheer waste. Nothing could be further from the truth! The religious life properly lived is a love at high

tension between God and the individual person. By consecrating their lives to Christ, religious trade the things of this
world for the riches of His love.

Priests, brothers and sisters who are loyal to their vocation cannot help being joyful, living so close to God and in
the great hope of the eternal reward promised to those who
leave all things in order to follow Jesus Christ. Gloomy,
narrow-minded people are not wanted in religious life. They
would become useless burdens in the manifold activities
that characterize every religious order or congregation in
the Church.

The Church loves all her children, but she wants her
priests, brothers and sisters to be energetic, humorous,
generous people who are also capable, sincere, faithful and
unselfish in their service of Christ.

taking that "fling at life"

Another mistaken idea which some have is that young
people should "try life" before entering religious life. This
is dangerous. By "taking a fling at life," many a young person
has lost his or her vocation and regretted it later on.

Others who "took a fling" have not lost the vocation, but
nevertheless regretted their lack of prudence. Laying oneself
open to many temptations is not the best way to prepare for
religious life. It is wrong to "test" one's vocation by exposing
it to every danger. Do gardeners test the hardiness of little
plants by setting them out in rough weather before they have
had time to acquire the necessary strength to withstand the
wind and the storm?

Young people with vocations are like those little plants;
they must guard carefully against the rough weather of temptations.

Modesty is the greatest protection, for modesty foresees
what would be an occasion of sin and refuses to take chances
with temptation.

It is true that many religious took their "fling at life,"
but because of it they had more slums to tear down before
they could begin to build the cathedral of sanctity once they
started the "upward climb." Those who are excellent are
excellent despite their "fling," not because of it.

From this follows the wisdom of answering a call to
religious life while one is young, still in high school for
instance, even though there are many who think otherwise.

There are still religious orders which have a fully accredited Juniorate and accept candidates of high school age.

God is welcomed and works freely in the soul of such a young person. Out of one thousand religious in over fifty-one orders asked about their vocation, two hundred and ninety said they had known of their vocation before the age of ten, three hundred and forty four, between the ages of ten and fifteen. This presents a total of six hundred and thirty-four, or more than three fifths of the group interviewed!

A young adult who thinks he or she might have a religious vocation should ask for the strength to do God's will, praying especially to Mary, the great mother and queen of religious. He or she should also go to Mass, Communion and confession often and practice generosity by doing "something extra" for someone every day, even when it requires sacrifice of some little enjoyment. The "final touch" will be to read inspiring biographies of men and women who consecrated their lives to God and made a success of it!

parents of religious —

God Himself a debtor to them

Without a doubt, parents feel the sacrifice when a beloved son or daughter is called to consecrate his or her life entirely to God. However, mother and father reflect that this is a supreme honor to their family. A special reward in heaven awaits such mothers and fathers, for God considers Himself a debtor to them.

If the son or daughter called to religious life is an only child, the merit and reward of the parents will be so much the greater, since their sacrifice is greater. Generally, the vocations which cost more sacrifice are the ones which bear the most fruit.

Lovable "Mamma Marguerita," the widowed mother of St. John Bosco, is a moving example. When her son would ask for advice about his choice of state in life, Margaret would answer, "I desire nothing of you except this: that you save your soul." Then John made up his mind to become a priest.

The pastor, knowing that Margaret was poor and a widow, thought it best to warn her.

Later she spoke to John saying, "Our pastor came and told me that you would like to become a priest. I only desire that you examine yourself well and think of the step you would like to take; then follow your vocation without thinking of me.

First of all comes the salvation of your soul. The pastor would like me to dissuade you in view of my needs. I tell you that when dealing with vocations, God is everything.... I expect nothing from you. I was born poor and I am poor; I desire to die poor." So John (Don) Bosco became a priest, a religious, and the founder of a great religious congregation helping thousands and thousands of boys.

children are God's first...

Just as a decision to enter a certain state in life cannot be forced upon anyone, so also no one should be prevented from following a vocation as long as he or she can meet the requirements. To select one's state in life as well as to choose one's marriage partner is the natural right of every person. Children belong first to God, then to their parents.

Mother or father would never want to stand in the way of God's plans and see their child follow a state in life unsuited for him, or worse yet, fall into serious vice and break their hearts. Parents would certainly not want to be deprived of the many temporal and spiritual graces which God showers upon the generous, especially those who offer Him their own flesh and blood.

The following letter was written by a father to his only daughter in the convent:

Dear Sister Patricia,

Your letter of January 9, as always, made me very happy. I could just picture you on Christmas Eve and imagine your happiness! Coupled with the picture referred to above was just a wee bit of envy! Surely you have not been removed from things long enough to have forgotten that such genuine joy as you described is rare indeed in the "outside world." God has been so good to you, dear; I sincerely hope you thank Him every day of your life.

And when I reflect that Mom and I had some small part to play in your ultimate choice of a vocation, it makes me very happy, too. I can safely tell you now—after a lapse of nearly three years—that there were times when I was gravely troubled as to what to say and how to advise "my little girl." Appreciating well the scholastic gifts with which you have been endowed and the scholarships available to you, and having a fatherly pride in your past accomplishments while anticipating others to come, there were times when I was strongly tempted to dissuade you from your course of action.

I thank God that He gave me the grace to realize the essential selfishness of my reasoning. In the light of the above you can imagine my joy when I receive a letter like your last one and appreciate in all its fullness the wisdom of your choice and the working of God's grace in my acquiescence. Would that all parents might experience my joy as I read your last letter! There would be few instances of parental opposition to religious vocations.

God love you always,
Dad

golden words

"Our heart is not free from great anxiety," wrote Pope Paul VI. "There are too many empty places in the framework of the services which the Church needs. The number of vocations is too scanty in proportion to the needs. And we will go further, it is too scanty in proportion to the possibilities for the ministry. At times, this or that community of the faithful appears too indifferent to the problem of recruitment and formation of the clergy for our heart to be placated.

"We wish we could reach the doorways of the homes of many Christian families with a distinct but frank word: Do you have any vocations among your children?

"We wish we could reach every pastor, every spiritual teacher: Are you watchful to discover the signs of a divine calling among the persons entrusted to your care?

"And then, like the messengers of the Gospel word on the roads of the world, we would like to say to youth, among all the rest: Do you know that Christ needs you? Do you know that His call is for the strong; that it is for those who rebel against mediocrity and the cowardice of a comfortable and insignificant life; that it is for those who maintain an understanding of the Gospel and feel the duty to regenerate the ecclesiastical life with their own personal contribution and by bearing the cross?

"May our cry be heard! But, meanwhile, we ask all, yes, all of you members of the holy Church of God, to welcome our invitation and to do at least one thing: do what Christ Himself commanded: 'Pray...the Lord of the harvest that He send forth laborers into His harvest' (Mt. 9:38)."

Young men and women—Christ's work of bringing to all men the light of the Gospel is not finished. To all Christians, especially to priests and religious, belongs the privilege of cooperating with Christ in the salvation of the world. Do you dare to get involved in advancing the cause of Christ?

WHAT THEY ASK
ABOUT THE STATES

A young adult should consider each state in life with its particular requirements, then take into account his like and dislikes, abilities and inclinations. He must see if he is drawn to a particular state and if he has the qualities demanded for success and contentment in that state.

1. *Can one become a saint in any walk of life?*

In the Church, there are holy people of all different professions, ages and conditions of life. Never before, you might say, as in these times, has there been such a splendid array of chosen souls! Pontifical giants of holiness such as Pius X, Pius XII, John XXIII; holy bishops such as Cardinals Stepinac, Mindszenty and Bishop Walsh of Maryknoll; zealous priests like Father Flannagan of Boys' Town, Father Keller and Father Matthew Crawley; devout men in public life who lived by high ideals such as Alfred E. Smith and John F. Kennedy; souls of total dedication to the service of their fellow men such as Doctor Tom Dolley; writers such as Joyce Kilmer; workers like the ex-alcoholic Matt Talbot, and "Mary's waiter", Italy's Joseph Rivella; lay apostles such as Edel Quinn; Sodalists like Mary Ellen Kelly; missionaries such as Father Damien and Mother Cabrini; religious like St. Therese the Little Flower, Brother Andre, Edith Stein and Father Maximilian Kolbe; children such as St. Dominic Savio and St. Maria Goretti.

2. *What kind of apostolic activity can the layman do?*

The laity have many marvelous opportunities for apostolic activity in such fields as church communities, the family, youth, the social milieu, and in national and international spheres. One can engage in apostolic activity either as an individual or as a member of an apostolic group.

3. *What very valuable apostolate can a layman perform as an individual?*

An individual layman can always perform the apostolate of good example. His living testimony of a fervent Christian life is the best advertisement for Christ and His Church. From the statistics of conversions in pagan countries — for example, Japan — it is clear that the great majority of conversions do not come about through the efforts of missionaries alone, but also through the beautiful examples of Christian virtue and the evident joy of the converts themselves. And this is the very reason why Christianity spread so rapidly in the first decades of the Church.

4. *Is the lay apostolate* **needed** *or is it something "extra" in the Church?*

The Holy Fathers continually declare to different groups of people that the Church needs the lay apostles to work side by side with priests to re-Christianize their environment. The Council Fathers of Vatican II urge "all the laity in the Lord to answer gladly, nobly and promptly the more urgent invitation of Christ in this hour and the impulse of the Holy Spirit. Young people should feel that this call has been directed to them especially and they should respond to it eagerly and generously. Through this holy synod, the Lord renews His invitation to all the laity to come closer to Him every day, recognizing that what is His is also their own, to associate themselves with Him in His saving mission" (Decree on Apostolate of the Laity).

5. *Do you love your faith? Do you try, in your own little way, to spread it?*

St. Augustine asks:

"Have you ever saved a soul? Are you sure of saving yours? Have you ever tried to say a good word to bring someone back to the sacraments?"

Such joy, such enthusiasm the Christian apostolate excites in the heart. It means sacrifice, but at the end of the day, what satisfaction one feels! It seems as if Christ says in the depths of one's heart, "Wonderful! good and faithful servant! I am proud of you!"

Do you belong to some form of organized apostolate? Remember that the sacraments of Baptism and Confirmation bind you to the cause of Christ the King and make you a soldier in the holy battles of the Lord and of the Church.

We should pray to the Virgin to make us apostles, to instill in us an ardent thirst for souls, and a desire to help the Church bring the Divine Master Way, Truth and Life to every heart.

6. *Are all those who do not choose marriage automatically called to the religious life?*

In the fifth chapter of his Gospel, St. Mark tells us of a poor man, possessed by an evil spirit, who spent his days and nights in a graveyard near the mountains, shouting and beating himself with stones. After being miraculously freed by Jesus, the man, perhaps fearing to fall once again victim to the hateful power of Satan, or wishing to show gratitude to his benefactor, begged to be allowed to follow Jesus as His disciple. However, the Master, boarding a boat to go to another region, only answered: "Go home to your relatives, and tell them all that the Lord has done for you and how he has had mercy on you" (Mark 5:19).

And the man went, telling everyone in the Decapolis of the great things that Jesus had done. He became an apostle in the entire region beyond the Jordan.

This episode shows us clearly that the Lord does not permit everyone to follow Him in the religious life or in the priesthood. Many must remain in the world and carry out their apostolate in the midst of society. By forming a family? At times not even this is possible. There can be many circumstances determining the renunciation of one state or another.

If the Christian sees the hand of God in every event, the hand which governs everything with Providence and love, so much the more should he realize that this loving hand guides his own life. Let him be convinced that God arranges everything for a higher and eternal good.

7. How do we compare virginity and matrimony?

"Let him who chooses virginity not hold of little value or despise matrimony. Matrimony is good and virginity is better; matrimony's goal is noble, that of virginity, as the Gospel attests, is much higher, because virginity is embraced for love of Christ and is made productive by the fruit of charity. Above all, perpetual virginity is a pure host offered to God, a holy victim; and besides it is a flower which gives honor and joy to the Church, and is a great source of strength which the Church cannot exclude nor neglect" (Pope Pius XII, allocution to Discalced Carmelites).

8. Is the higher excellence of virginity and celibacy a doctrine of our faith?

"The higher excellence of virginity and celibacy, compared with the married state, is, as We have already noted, a doctrine taught in the first instance by our Divine Savior and by the Apostle of the Gentiles. It was solemnly defined as an article of divine faith by the Holy Council of Trent. It has always been taught by the Fathers and Doctors of the Church. Like Our Predecessors before Us, We Ourselves have taken every possible opportunity to expound the doctrine and to give it Our warm endorsement" (Pope Pius XII, Holy Virginity).

9. Is chastity an easy thing to guard in our life and with our nature?

"Keep well in mind that perfect chastity, and conjugal chastity also, cannot be preserved constantly without the aid of God's grace and this heavenly aid is even more necessary when it is a matter of preserving chastity until the last breath of life. Therefore, he who has made a vow to God of virginal integrity must struggle with prayer and with the exercise of penance, as Jacob with the angel, so as to be always victorious" (Pope Pius XII, Holy Virginity).

10. *What is the purpose of celibacy?*

"The teaching of Christ already suggests that lifelong celibacy frees people from the heavy cares and responsibilities of married life. The Apostle of the Gentiles, divinely inspired, tells in the following passage why celibacy is a liberation: 'And I would have you free from concern.... The married man is concerned with the world's claim, asking how he is to please his wife; and thus he is at issue with himself' (1 Cor. 7:32-33). But here it must be noted that the Apostle is not blaming husbands because they are concerned with their wives. Nor is he taking wives to task for trying to please their husbands. He is merely pointing out that their hearts are divided between love of the partner and love of God, that they are too distracted by the anxieties and obligations of married life to be able readily to give their minds to the affairs of God. They are subject to the duty of wedlock, which clearly commands that 'the two become one flesh' (Matt. 19:5). Man and wife are joined together in all the gladdening and saddening circumstances of their lives. Hence it will readily be appreciated why those who wish to give themselves to the service of God embrace the state of virginity as a state of emancipation, which enables them to serve God more completely and to devote their undivided energies to the welfare of their fellowmen" (Pope Pius XII, Holy Virginity).

11. *Is priestly celibacy still advocated in our times?*

Vatican Council II said:

"Perfect and perpetual continence for the sake of the kingdom of heaven, commended by Christ the Lord (cf. Matt. 19:22) and through the course of time as well as in our own days, freely accepted and observed in a praiseworthy manner by many of the faithful, is held by the Church to be of great value in a special manner for the priestly life....

"Indeed celibacy has a many-faceted suitability for the priesthood. For the whole priestly mission is dedicated to the service of a new humanity which Christ, the victor over death, has aroused through His Spirit in the world and which has its origin 'not of blood, nor of the will of the flesh, nor of the will of man, but of God' (John 1:13)" (Decree on the Ministry and Life of Priests, n. 16).

12. Did Christ choose the celibate life?

"Christ, the only Son of the Father, by the power of the Incarnation itself, was made Mediator between heaven and earth, between the Father and the human race. Wholly in accord with this mission, Christ remained throughout His whole life in the state of celibacy, which signified His total dedication to the service of God and men. This deep connection between celibacy and the priesthood of Christ is reflected in those whose fortune it is to share in the dignity and in the mission of the Mediator and eternal Priest; this sharing will be more perfect the freer the sacred minister is from the bonds of flesh and blood" (Priestly Celibacy, 21).

13. Is chastity harmful to physical and mental equilibrium?

"In the first place, people who regard man's natural sex instinct as the dominant factor in his make-up, and infer from this that he can master it for a lifetime only at the imminent peril of upsetting his physical and, still more, his mental equilibrium, with consequent harm to the balance of his human personality, are simply going counter to the common judgment of sane and conscientious men, for which the Church has ever entertained the greatest respect.

"As St. Thomas so justly and rightly states, the most deep-seated of all human instincts is the instinct of self-preservation, whereas the sex instinct lies on a more superficial level. It belongs to the controlling power of human reason, which is the singular prerogative of our nature, to govern these fundamental impulses and to sublimate them by exercising due mastery over them" (Pope Pius XII, Holy Virginity).

14. How does the practice of perfect chastity develop one's personality?

"In order to acquire this perfect sway over our bodily passions, it is not enough to refrain from any direct violation of chastity. Willing and generous avoidance of everything that is more or less distantly opposed to the practice of this virtue is indispensable. Then the soul can completely rule the body and lead the life of the spirit in peace and freedom. Anyone, therefore, who acts on Catholic principles cannot fail to see that, far from arresting the natural progressive

development of men and women, perfect chastity furthers
and ennobles it to the highest degree" (Holy Virginity).

15. *Is it true that the mutual assistance in matrimony is
a better aid to self-sanctification than the celibate's call?*

"It cannot be asserted, as some would have it, that the
mutual assistance which the parties look for in marriage is a
better aid to self-sanctification than what they call the virgin's
or celibate's 'loneliness of heart.' For, despite their renunciation of this particular kind of human love, it is not true to
say that those who have embraced the state of perfect chastity
have thereby dwarfed and denuded their human personality.
They receive from God, the Giver of gifts descending from
above, something in the spiritual order which utterly transcends the 'mutual assistance' rendered to each other by man
and wife. As they give themselves entirely to the One who is
the source of their being and who imparts to them His divine
love, they are not contracted but amplified to a degree. Those
wonderful words of St. Paul: 'I live, now, not I; it is Christ
that lives in me' (Gal. 2:20)—can anyone apply them to himself with more justice than these virgins?" (Pope Pius XII,
Holy Virginity).

16. *What about those who say that married couples can
do more good in the world than consecrated virgins?*

"We also deem it expedient to refer to another mistake,
the mistake made by advisers who wish to discourage young
men from entering seminaries and young women from entering convents, by trying to make them believe that the Church
of today stands in greater need of the help that can be given
by good practicing Catholics living an ordinary married life
in the world than of priests and nuns who are supposed to
be withdrawn from human society by their vows of chastity.
This is nothing but palpable and dangerous make-believe"
(Pope Pius XII, Holy Virginity).

17. *If we look back into history at the towering deeds of
celibate saints, can we easily see the worth and reason for
consecrated virginity?*

"How, for example, could a missionary such as the wonderful St. Francis Xavier, a father of the poor such as the
merciful St. Vincent de Paul, a zealous educator of youth
like St. John Bosco, a tireless 'mother of emigrants' like
St. Francis Xavier Cabrini, have accomplished such gigantic
and painful labors, if each had to look after the corporal and
spiritual needs of a wife or a husband and children?" (Pope
Pius XII, Holy Virginity).

18. *Of what is virginity consecrated to Christ a proof?*

"Virginity consecrated to Christ is in itself such an evidence of faith in the kingdom of heaven, such a proof of love for our Divine Redeemer, that there is little wonder if it bears abundant fruits of sanctity. Innumerable are the virgins and apostles vowed to perfect chastity who are the honor of the Church by the lofty sanctity of their lives. In truth, virginity gives souls a force of spirit capable of leading them even to martyrdom, if needs be; such is the clear lesson of history which proposes a whole host of virgins to our admiration, from Agnes of Rome to Maria Goretti" (Pope Pius XII, Holy Virginity).

19. *What message does the religious life give to the world?*

"The religious state clearly manifests that the kingdom of God and its needs, in a very special way, are raised above all earthly considerations. It clearly shows all men both the unsurpassed breadth of the strength of Christ the King and the infinite power of the Holy Spirit marvelously working in the Church" (Dogmatic Constitution on the Church, n. 44).

20. *Is religious life a "divine call" or is it a career one chooses like law, medicine, social work, etc.?*

The Second Vatican council declared:

"Members of each Institute should recall first of all that by professing the evangelical counsels they responded to *a divine call* so that, by being not only dead to sin but also renouncing the world, they may live for God alone. They have dedicated their entire lives to His service. *This constitutes a special consecration, which is deeply rooted in that of Baptism and expresses it more fully*" (Decree on the Adaptation and Renewal of Religious Life, n. 5).

21. *Does the religious priest, brother or sister, have a model to imitate?*

"The pursuit of perfect charity through the evangelical counsels draws its origin from the doctrine and example of *the Divine Master* and reveals itself as a splendid sign of the heavenly kingdom" (Decree on the Adaptation and Renewal of Religious Life, n. 1).

22. *Why is the profession of religious vows important?*

"The importance of the profession of the evangelical counsels is seen in the fact that it fosters the perfection of love of God and love of neighbor in an outstanding manner and that this profession is strengthened by vows" (Dogmatic Constitution on the Church, n. 45).

23. *Is it easier to practice virtue in the religious life?*

"This service of God ought to inspire and foster in religious the exercise of the virtues, especially humility, obedience, fortitude and chastity. In such a way they share in Christ's emptying of Himself and His life in the spirit.

"Faithful to their profession then, and leaving all things for the sake of Christ, religious are to follow Him as the one thing necessary, listening to His words and solicitous for the things that are His" (Decree on the Adaptation and Renewal of Religious Life, n. 5).

24. *In what great virtue should religious be outstanding?*

"*Let those who make profession of the evangelical counsels seek and love above all else God who has first loved us* and let them strive to foster in all circumstances a life hidden with Christ in God. This love of God both excites and energizes that love of one's neighbor which contributes to the salvation of the world and the building up of the Church. This love, in addition, quickens and directs the actual practice of the evangelical counsels" (Decree on the Adaptation and Renewal of Religious Life, n. 6).

25. *What is the value of the religious vow of chastity?*

"The chastity 'for the sake of the kingdom of heaven' (Matt. 19:12) which religious profess should be counted an outstanding gift of grace. It frees the heart of man in a unique fashion so that it may be more inflamed with love for God and for all men. Thus it not only symbolizes in a singular way the heavenly goods, but also the most suitable means by which religious dedicate themselves with undivided heart to the service of God and the works of the apostolate. In this way they recall to the minds of all the faithful the wondrous marriage decreed by God and which is to be fully revealed in the future age in which the Church takes Christ as its only Spouse" (Decree on the Adaptation and Renewal of Religious Life, n. 12).

26. *How is the vow of poverty related to the following of Christ?*

"Religious should diligently practice and if need be express also in new forms that voluntary poverty which is recognized and highly esteemed especially today as an expression of the following of Christ. By it they share in the poverty of Christ who for our sakes became poor, even though He was rich, so that by His poverty we might become rich" (Decree on the Adaptation and Renewal of Religious Life, n. 13).

27. *What does the vow of religious obedience entail?*

"In professing obedience, religious offer the full sur-render of their own will as a sacrifice of themselves to God and so are united permanently and securely to God's salvific will" (Decree on the Adaptation and Renewal of Religious Life, n. 14).

28. *If the religious life is "the following of Christ" why then is the vow of obedience so important?*

"After the example of Jesus Christ who came to do the will of the Father and 'assuming the nature of a slave' (Phil. 2:7) learned obedience in the school of suffering, religious under the motion of the Holy Spirit, subject themselves in faith to their superiors who hold the place of God. Under their guidance they are led to serve all their brothers in Christ, just as Christ Himself in obedience to the Father served His brethren and laid down His life as a ransom for many. So they are closely bound to the service of the Church and strive to attain the measure of the full manhood of Christ" (Decree on the Adaptation and Renewal of Religious Life, n. 14).

29. *What is the "common life" in religious orders? What are its benefits? Is it still in* **vogue** *today or can religious now go on their own and do what they want?*

"Common life, fashioned on the model of the early Church where the body of believers was united in heart and soul, and given new force by the teaching of the Gospel, the sacred liturgy and especially the Eucharist, should continue to be lived in prayer and the communion of the same spirit. As members of Christ living together as brothers, religious should give pride of place in esteem to each other and bear each other's burdens. For the community, a true family gathered together in the name of the Lord by God's love which has flooded the hearts of its members through the Holy Spirit, rejoices because He is present among them" (Decree on the Adaptation and Renewal of Religious Life, n. 15).

30. *Who makes the laws for religious orders? Can each individual religious do what he or she feels best?*

"It is the duty of the ecclesiastical hierarchy to regulate the practice of the evangelical counsels by law, since it is the duty of the same hierarchy to care for the People of God and to lead them to the most fruitful pastures" (Dogmatic Constitution on the Church, n. 45).

31. *Is* **prayer** *the center of all-religious life no matter the specific apostolate?*

"Drawing upon the authentic sources of Christian spirituality, members of religious communities should resolutely cultivate both the spirit and practice of prayer. In the first place they should have recourse daily to the Holy Scriptures in order that, by reading and meditating on Holy Writ, they may learn 'the surpassing worth of knowing Jesus Christ' (Phil. 3:8). They should celebrate the sacred liturgy, especially the holy sacrifice of the Mass, with both lips and heart as the Church desires and so nourish their spiritual life from this richest of sources" (Decree on the Adaptation and Renewal of Religious Life, n. 6).

32. *What are the results of prayer in the life of a religious?*

"So refreshed at the table of divine law and the sacred altar of God, they will love Christ's members as brothers, honor and love their pastors as sons should do, and living and thinking ever more in union with the Church, dedicate themselves wholly to its mission" (Decree on the Adaptation and Renewal of Religious Life, n. 6).

33. *How can a good religious be of great inspiration to all?*

"Religious should carefully keep before their minds the fact that the Church presents Christ to believers and nonbelievers alike in a striking manner daily through them. The Church thus portrays Christ in contemplation on the mountain, in His proclamation of the kingdom of God to the multitudes, in His healing of the sick and maimed, in His work of converting sinners to a better life, in His solicitude for youth and His goodness to all men, always obedient to the will of the Father who sent Him" (Dogmatic Constitution on the Church, n. 46).

34. *Do religious help the world and those who live in it?*

"Let no one think that religious have become strangers to their fellowmen or useless citizens of this earthly city by their consecration. For even though it sometimes happens that religious do not directly mingle with their contemporaries, yet in a more profound sense these same religious are united with them in the heart of Christ and spiritually cooperate with them. In this way the building up of the earthly city may have its foundation in the Lord and may tend toward Him, lest perhaps those who build this city shall have labored in vain" (Dogmatic Constitution on the Church, n. 46).

35. *Are there* **saints in the making** *among the men of today? Among consecrated souls today?*

"We are painfully aware of the shortcomings of some among us, the excesses of a few. There is neither possibility of concealing these nor point to apology for them. But we can and do ask that people, beginning with people within the Church, be more mindful of our saints, notably the saints in the making among our priests. The Church never promised to be without sinners and she is the last to repudiate them; it was promised that she would give the world many and great saints. In this time of adjustment and self-scrutiny, God is faithful to His promise to raise up in our midst the saints He has never denied us. Future generations may yet envy us the opportunities for sanctity we had and the number of saints God gave us, especially those American priests and religious who do far more good than they realize, even if it be less than, in their zeal, they intend" (The Church in Our Day, American Bishops).

EACH OF US

1. *Since my life is a gift from God, what important points must I consider and weigh as the road of my future unravels before me?*

a) Each one of us has his own personal vocation, a place all his own in the immense organism of society. Each one's task is assigned him directly by God, who gives certain inclinations and abilities, according to His unsearchable designs, calling some to one state in life, some to another.

b) All positions, the lowest as well as the highest, can be useful and meritorious before God and before society, depending upon the spirit of those who exercise them. For over thirty years our Lord fulfilled the humble and fatiguing work of a carpenter. And the beads of His perspiration were joined in the work of our Redemption to the blood He shed.

c) God knows our desires and our potentialities. He knows the amount of good that He can reap from His creatures. The call of God tends precisely to put each individual in the place that best permits him to take full advantage of his abilities, for his own happiness and that of all society.

2. *How can we show our thanks to the good God for His tremendous gift of life?*

Be truly grateful to the Lord for the many gifts and graces He has showered upon you—intelligence, health, Christian education.... Without envying your friends, pray and try to find out what God's plans are for you, for each of us has a mission to accomplish on earth.

Try to diligently fulfill your duties day by day.

As God prepared Mary with privileges and special graces for her great mission of bringing Jesus to the world, He also prepares each of us with talents and graces for our particular state in life. It is up to us to use God's gifts and graces advantageously.

The Second Vatican Council's Challenge to Young Adults

The Second Vatican Council's challenge to young adults:
"It is to you, young men and women of the world, that the Council wishes to address its final message. For it is you who are to receive the torch from the hands of your elders and to live in the world at the period of the most gigantic transformations ever realized in its history. It is you who, receiving the best of the example of the teaching of your parents and your teachers, are to form the society of tomorrow. You will either save yourselves or you will perish with it.

"The Church has been working to rejuvenate her image in order to respond the better to the design of her Founder, the great Living One, the Christ who is eternally young. At the term of this imposing re-examination of life, she now turns to you. It is for you, youth, especially for you that the Church now comes through her Council to enkindle your light, the light which illuminates the future, *your future*. The Church is anxious that this society that you are going to build up should respect the dignity, the liberty and the rights of individuals. *These individuals are you.*

"The Church is particularly anxious that this society should allow free expansion to her treasure ever ancient and ever new, namely faith, and that your souls may be able to bask freely in its helpful light. She has confidence that you will find such strength and such joy that you will not be tempted, as were some of your elders, to yield to the seductions of egoistic or hedonistic philosophies or to those of despair and annihilation, and that in the face of atheism, a phenomenon of lassitude and old age, you will know how to affirm your faith in life and in what gives meaning to life, that is to say, the certitude of the existence of a just and good God.

"It is in the name of this God and of His Son, Jesus, that we exhort you to open your hearts to the dimensions of the world, to heed the appeal of your brothers, to place your youthful energies at their service. Fight against all egoism.

Refuse to give free course to the instincts of violence and hatred which beget wars and all their train of miseries. Be generous, pure, respectful and sincere, and build in enthusiasm a better world than your elders had.

"The Church looks to you with confidence and with love. Rich with a long past of ever living in her, and marching on toward human perfection in time and the ultimate destinies of history and of life, the Church is the real youth of the world. She possesses what constitutes the strength and the charm of youth, that is to say, the ability to rejoice with what is beginning, to give oneself unreservedly, to renew one's self and to set out again for new conquests.

Look upon the Church and you will find in her the face of Christ, the genuine, humble and wise Hero, the prophet of truth and love, the companion and friend of youth. It is in the name of Christ that we salute you, that we exhort and bless you."

pattern your life after the

"greats"

AFRICA OR DEATH by Rev. A. G. Mondini, F.S.C.J. A dramatic re-telling of the events in the heroic life of the dedicated missionary, Bishop Comboni, founder of the Verona Fathers, whose motto was "Africa or Death!" 336 pages; Cloth $4; Paper $3

CALL ME JOHN by Richard Cardinal Cushing. "Captures the magnetic attraction of the late Holy Father" *The Indicator*. "John in this book is never alone but always *with* people in our Lord, ever gently tugging humanity's sleeve toward unity" *America*. 168 pages; Cloth $4; Paper $3

CHATS WITH POPE PAUL by J.L. Gonzalez. Fascinating personal insights into the mind and past of Paul VI based on the recollections of his closest friends. 192 pages; Cloth $4

CHRIST, HOPE OF THE WORLD by Igino Giordani. A new and vibrant life of Christ, overflowing with timely and profound insights. Full color illustrations. 480 pages; Cloth $7; Paper $5

A DEAN OF BOYS WRITES by Arthur V. Shea, S.J. Drawing on his years of varied and practical experiences as the Dean of Boys in an outstanding American University, Father Shea has composed a highly readable volume addressed to Dads and Deans and all those involved with modern teens. 151 pages; Cloth $3; Paper $2

FRIENDS OF GOD — FRIENDS OF MINE by Richard Cardinal Cushing. With striking originality and freshness of approach, the eminent author presents a wondrous gallery of profiles — scientists, musicians, diplomats, missionaries, politicians. His Eminence has written of these friends of God with the explicit purpose of injecting some of their spirit into our daily lives. 256 pages; Cloth $3.50 Paper $2.50

GOOD FATHER IN BRITTANY by Rev. M. P. Harney, S.J. The life of Blessed Julien Maunoir, apostle of Brittany, a pioneer in the techniques of audio-visual education and a proposed patron for the CCD! 328 pages; Cloth $5; Paper $4

HERO OF MOLOKAI by Rev. Omer Englebert. The gripping story of Father Damian, apostle of the lepers, by a well-known author. Filled with thrills, pathos and intense human interest, Father Damian's story is unforgettable. Illustrated. 364 pages; Cloth $3; Paper $2

JOHN F. KENNEDY, AMERICAN by Charles Dollen. "This informal biography of John F. Kennedy was written primarily for young readers and is recommended as a valuable edition for any high school library" *Best Sellers*. 244 pages; Cloth $5.00; Paper $4.00

THE LAWYER IN COMMUNISM — Memoirs of a Lawyer Behind the Iron Curtain by Dr. Lajos Kálmán. With a foreword by Richard Cardinal Cushing. 196 pages; Cloth $3; Paper $2

LOUIS MARTIN, AN IDEAL FATHER, St. Theresa's Father by L. and M. Wust. "A wise and interesting book...a valuable addition to the literature of Theresiana" *The Register*. 347 pages; Cloth $3; Paper $1.50

OUR LADY'S KNIGHT by Rev. Lawrence Lovasik, S.V.D. The heartwarming story of Technical Sergeant Leo E. Lovasik (1921-1943), who, with undaunted courage and joy, gave his heart to his Queen of the Skies, and his life to his country. 232 pages; Cloth $3; Paper $2

SAINTS FOR THE MODERN WOMAN by Rev. Luke Farley. This book brings to the fore the modern woman's very real call to holiness by introducing her to some of her feminine predecessors in sanctity;

Order from addresses at the back of this book.

women like herself from every century and walk of life. 264 pages; Cloth $3.95; Paper $2.50

WOMAN OF FAITH by the Daughters of St. Paul. Presents the image of a really modern nun—a profile of the Servant of God, Mother Thecla Merlo, Co-Foundress of the Daughters of St. Paul. Every page will prove for the reader an illuminating discovery of how Christian involvement with our modern world goes hand in hand with the perfection of charity and love of God. 226 pages; Cloth $3; Paper $2

THE WORLD'S CARDINAL by M. C. Devine. First full length biography of Richard Cardinal Cushing. "The author has captured the prince who lives as a pauper, the reluctant celebrity who would rather have been a missionary" *The Pilot.* 356 pages; Cloth $5.75; Paper $4.75

ZELIE MARTIN, Mother of the Little Flower by Louis and Marjorie Wust. Making use of Mrs. Martin's heretofore unavailable personal letters, the authors have produced an impressive biography of an extraordinary wife and mother of nine saintly children. 300 pages; Cloth $5; Paper $4

what shall I be?

vocation

career

THE AGE OF LAY SANCTITY by Richard Cardinal Cushing. The most realistic program today is the program "to restore all things to Christ." 16 pages; 15c

CATHOLIC VOCATION IN JOURNALISM by Richard Cardinal Cushing. "The distinction between a Catholic journalist and the journalist who is Catholic is the awareness of the power for doing good which trademarks such a vocation." 16 pages; 15c

CHOOSE YOUR TOMORROW by the Daughters of St. Paul. It is important to face life squarely and sensibly, to choose the right path, the one which God Himself has established for happiness and eternal salvation. "Each of us has a place," "Everyone is called to happiness," "Love is the answer," "Family life," "Virginity in the world," "Toward religious profession." "Our response is free"—these and other intriguing chapters will help young people choose their tomorrow. They will help them to understand how valuable life is when it is spent for an ideal, in the full light of our true destiny. 240 pages; Cloth $2; Paper $1

CHRIST IS HERE by the Daughters of St. Paul. The contemplative-active life and mission of the Daughters of St. Paul captured in picture and prose in a smartly

designed volume. 96 pages; Cloth $2; Paper $1

COME, FOLLOW ME by Richard Cardinal Cushing. A discussion of the religious vocation in general and of the belated vocation. 70 pages; 35c

HANDS THAT CARE by Richard Cardinal Cushing. A moving exhortation to dedicated, loving care of the afflicted—for nurses and all those whose hands serve others. 16 pages; 15c

HAVE I CHOSEN YOU? by Rev. Alfred M. Murphy, O.S.A. This book presents practical guidelines for the advancement of the spiritual lives of teenagers. 72 pages; 55c

HE SPEAKS TO YOU by Rev. Camillo Zamboni. Intimate heart to heart messages from Christ to the modern Miss. 196 pages; Paper 95c

A LOOK AT PSYCHIATRY by Richard Cardinal Cushing. A penetrating discussion of the need for mankind to draw from the eternal values courage and confidence with which to meet inevitable, day-to-day anxieties. 16 pages; 15c

THE MEN IN BLACK by Rev. Erminio Crippa, S.C.J. Informative and enjoyable

be informed —

ecumenical reading

Bishop of Worcester, Mass. 104 pages; Paper 60c; Pamphlet form 35c

HUMAN LIFE IN OUR DAY. A collective Pastoral Letter by the Bishops of the United States, commenting on the encyclical, *Humanae Vitae* of Paul VI. 25c

THE CHURCH—LIGHT OF ALL MANKIND by Pope Paul VI. The book begins with a discussion of ecumenism: the proper attitude to be taken, and the errors to be avoided. Other talks deal with the nature, marks, and missionary vocation of the Church; the mission of the laity, the proper balance between concern for the world and the necessary detachment of the Christian whose goal is beyond this world; devotion to the Holy Spirit and its relationship to respect for the visible Church; the importance of austerity, mortification and obedience to the vitality of the Church; and other matters of similar relevance. 156 pages; Cloth $2; Paper $1

CREED OF A CATHOLIC by Rev. Wilfred Hurley, C.S.P. "As a man thinks, so he is." Catholics think and live according to a Creed. This is the story of that Creed. 153 pages; Cloth $3; Paper $2

CHRIST THE ANSWER by Rev. Peter Sullivan. An appealing and interesting book of apologetics stressing the implication of the divinity of Christ for the modern world. "Valuable reading for the layman or the person involved in CCD work" *Anton Wamback, S.D.S.* 272 pages; Cloth $4; Paper $3

FAITH—RESPONSE TO THE DIALOGUE OF GOD by Pope Paul VI. This book contains fifteen addresses of Pope Paul VI, all of them having to do with some aspect of faith, and with the revivifying of Christian life that was contemplated by the Council. The talks deal with such matters as the need for interior grace; the relation of faith and good works; erroneous opinions regarding defined truths of the faith; the continuing need for spiritual progress; heroes of the faith. 144 pages; Cloth $2; Paper $1

DOCUMENTS OF VATICAN II. The 16 documents of Vatican II in compact paperback; the official text of all the documents complete with *footnotes* and *topical index*. This valuable edition, immensely practical, is also enriched with direct commentaries from outstanding Council Fathers. Paper $1.25

personality growth

THE SACRAMENTS by Richard Cardinal Cushing. Absorbing stories and illuminating discussions point up the treasures of the sacramental system for teenagers as well as for adults. Fully treated are the role of frequent Communion in the struggle against temptation, the meaning of vocation, dating and courtship. 224 pages; Cloth $3; Paper $2

SPIRITUAL GUIDEPOSTS by Richard Cardinal Cushing. The Ten Commandments in a style that will appeal to youth and to adults. A delightful blend of detailed explanations, practical guide rules, intriguing stories, sparkling humor and inspirational anecdotes. 192 pages; Cloth $3; Paper $2

THE PURPOSE OF LIVING by Richard Cardinal Cushing. A course of studies in a Catholic institution of higher learning among other things aims to make men realize that they are not merely natural men, but men who possess a supernatural destiny. 16 pages; 15c

RELIGION IN EDUCATION by Richard Cardinal Cushing. "The highly developed technology of our culture demands an educated people to operate it effectively. Knowledge without wisdom is a dangerous weapon; learning without religion and principles and ideals leads mankind into the worst aberrations" *America.* 16 pages; 15c

WOMAN: HER INFLUENCE AND ZEAL as an Aid to the Priesthood by Very Rev. James Alberione, S.S.P., S.T.D. "Father Alberione sets forth precisely what the Christian woman—regardless of her age or station—should be" *The Priest.* 316 pages; Cloth $3.50; Paper $2.50

WOMAN'S SUBLIME CALL by Rt. Rev. Paul V. Harrington. The author clarifies the true role of woman, particularly married woman, by correlating her creation by God with her marital responsibility. 90 pages; Cloth $1.50; Paper $1.00

DSP PAMPHLETS

A new series of pocket-sized pamphlets chock full of solid answers to timely questions. Perfect for parish pamphlet racks, discussion clubs, youth meetings or individual reading.

Faith Against Hope, 10c
The One Church, 10c
Peace of Mind through Mental Order, 10c
The Right To Be Wrong, 15c
So You've Got a Date, 10c
Supreme Honor for Parents, 10c

What Is Man? 10c
Love or Puppy Love 10c
What's My Line, 10c
Do You Have the Right Slant on Sex, 10c
Third Finger, Left Hand, 10c
Everybody Has Trouble, 10c
Hands That Held the Beads, 10c
In a Glass, Darkly, 10c
Who Is My Neighbor? 10c
My Problem Was Myself, 10c
The Credo of the People of God, 10c
On Human Life, *Humanae Vitae*, 15c

sociology

man and his world!

AN APPEAL TO ALL AMERICANS To Join the Battle Against Communism by Richard Cardinal Cushing. 16 pages; 15c

THE CHURCH AND COMMUNISM by Richard Cardinal Cushing. 16 pp.; 15c

CIVIL RIGHTS. A source book compiled by Rev. Charles Dollen. A compilation of the fundamental documents on this vital issue, drawn from Papal Encyclicals, documents of Vatican II, pronouncements of American Catholic Bishops, and Scripture, enriched with alphabetical and analytical indexes. 150 pages; Cloth $2; Paper $1

DESIGNS FOR PROGRESS by Leon McKenzie. A presentation of the core social teachings of the Church from Leo XIII to Paul VI in a manner that is comprehensive, relative and striking. Ideal for informative teen reading. Excellent "term paper" material. Cloth $2; Paper $1

FUNDAMENTALS OF CHRISTIAN SOCIOLOGY by Rev. James Alberione, S.S.P., S.T.D. "A good book for discussion clubs" *Today's Family.* "Today when the social question is discussed on all sides, there is need for such a book as this which offers a clear exposition of the principles in Christian social teaching" *The Catholic Book Review.* 188 pages; Cloth $2.50; Paper $1.50

INTER-RACIAL JUSTICE by Richard Cardinal Cushing. 16 pages; 10c

A SUMMONS TO RACIAL JUSTICE by Richard Cardinal Cushing. 24 pages; 6c

THE SECRET OF HER GREATNESS, U.S.A. by Rev. Clement H. Crock. A memorable analysis of the true reasons for America's greatness. 176 pages; Cloth $2.50; Paper $1.50

QUESTIONS AND ANSWERS ON COMMUNISM Booklet 1 by Richard Cardinal Cushing. *In simple understandable form.* This booklet is a practical question and answer explanation of the origins, tactics and goals of atheistic Communism. *Especially prepared for use in Elementary and Junior High Schools! Those with limited reading time will also find Booklet 1 profitable.* English, 64 pages; 50c; Spanish, 64 pages; 50c

QUESTIONS AND ANSWERS ON COMMUNISM Booklet 2 by Richard Cardinal Cushing. This is a valuable booklet for classes and study groups to equip them to oppose atheistic Communism intelligently. 248 pages; $1.25; available in Spanish, $1

ONE FAMILY UNDER GOD compiled by the Daughters of St. Paul. One is the community of all peoples, one their origin, for God made the whole human race to live over the face of the earth. One also is their final goal, God.

This timely, penetrating book contains: General principles laid down by Vatican II, Pope John XXIII, Pope Paul VI and the Bishops of the U.S.A. in order to meet the urgent needs of our age with a gallant and unified effort born of love. 104 pages; Cloth $2; Paper $1

CONFERENCES ON COMMUNISM by Richard Cardinal Cushing. 80 pages; 50c

scripture

THE NEW TESTAMENT. Confraternity text of the New Testament printed in large, clear type. Introductions before each book of the New Testament as well as numerous explanatory footnotes; bound in a strong, flexible binding. 384 pages; Cloth $1.75; Paper 95c

THE HOLY GOSPEL. Pocket-size. Confraternity edition. Apologetical footnotes – a unique arrangement of catechetical teachings about corresponding Gospel passages. Illustrated. 720 pages;

HOLY GOSPEL. Large print. Cloth $5; Paper $4

THE EPISTLES OF ST. PAUL. Confraternity edition. Illustrated. 245 pages; Paper $1

LET US PRAY WITH THE PSALMS. A handy-sized book for pocket or purse, containing selected psalms appropriate for prayers of adoration, petition, contrition, etc. 291 pages; Paper $1

Mary

MARY OF NAZARETH by Igino Giordani. Mary's story begins in eternity and continues on without interruption. It is the story of a miracle which God the Creator wrought for His own joy and that of the whole world. 181 pages; Cloth $5; Paper $4

MARY, HOPE OF THE WORLD by Very Rev. James Alberione, S.S.P., S.T.D. A brilliant consideration of Mary under three aspects: in the mind of God, in prophecies, and in the longing of humanity; in her earthly life as Co-redemptrix of mankind; and in her life of glory in heaven, in the Church and in the hearts of the faithful. 222 pages; Cloth $3; Paper $1.50

MARY, STAR OF THE SEA by Rev. Albert Barbieri, S.S.P. "St. Bernard's famous words concerning Mary, Star of the Sea, form the subject of these thirty-one lofty meditations on Marian instructions, illustrated by appropriate examples" Rev. Gabriel M. Roschini, O.S.M. 250 pp.; Cloth $3; Paper $2

MARY, MOTHER AND MODEL by Very Rev. James Alberione, S.S.P., S.T.D. The

appealing vision of Our Lady shining forth from thirty of her liturgical feasts. Learn the history and aim of each great Marian feast, its part in the Breviary, and the benefits to be derived from its observance. Illustrated. 237 pages; Cloth $3; Paper $1.50

GLORIES AND VIRTUES OF MARY by Very Rev. James Alberione, S.S.P., S.T.D. A moving presentation of Mary's heroic virtues and great privileges, drawn from Sacred Scripture and the Fathers of the Church. "Singular style, simple but thought-provoking" Sponsa Regis. 251 pages; Cloth $3; Paper $1.50

HAIL HOLY QUEEN by Rev. John H. Collins, S.J. Moving reflections on one of Our Lady's most beautiful prayers. Full-color illustrations. 80 pages; cloth $2; Paper $1

MARY by Richard Cardinal Cushing. A series of vibrant, warm reflections on Our Lady. Priests, religious and laity will discover here new reasons for a more intense Marian devotion. "Increases devotion to Mary, Mother and Model of Adorers" The Register. 160 pages; Cloth $2.50; Paper $1.50

spiritual reading a few minutes a day!

WHAT THE WORLD NEEDS by Victor L. Dux, O.S.B. Father Dux writes with a verve and enthusiasm that is contagious. What the World Needs is rich with sparkling humor and epigrammatic insights into

a host of everyday problems that confront all manner of Christians who realize that the world earnestly needs the example of their genuine Christian witness. 216 pages. Cloth $3; Paper $2

THE IMITATION OF CHRIST by Thomas a Kempis. 440 pages; Cloth, red edges $2; Paper, red edges $1

LITTLE TALKS ABOUT LIFE by Rev. Patrick Fontaine. A fascinating and cheering book overflowing with beautiful thought gems and heart-warming messages of encouragement for good living. 335 pages; Cloth $3; Paper $2

PRAY ALWAYS by Very Rev. James Alberione, S.S.P., S.T.D. A solid and fundamental explanation of the need and value of prayer, various methods of speaking with God and the reward of closer living with God in daily life. 264 pages; Cloth $3; Paper $2

PRAY LIKE THIS—PRAY WITH ST. PAUL by Rev. Leonard Sheil, S.J. "An experienced retreat master of Ireland has written this thoughtful and practical series of meditations for the laity. His purpose is to help Catholic men and women grow in their intimacy with Christ through the practice of mental prayer" *America.* 336 pages; Cloth $3; Paper $2

SO HIGH THE PRICE by P. J. Kelly, S.T.L. In these post-conciliar times of earnest seeking after spiritual renewal this compact volume on hell, relying on Scripture and the Fathers of the Church, does not leave one fearful and trembling, but leads to stronger resolutions to choose God and His heaven. 85 pages; Cloth $2; Paper $1

SPIRITUAL DIARY "...a work nearly 200 years old, treats of 12 virtues, one for each month of the year. Under each virtue you will find 30 or more sayings and pithy comments from the writings and example of the saints and holy men" *Spiritual Book News.* 276 pages; Cloth $3; Paper $2

DAUGHTERS OF ST. PAUL

In Massachusetts
   50 St. Paul's Avenue
      Boston, Mass. 02130
   172 Tremont Street
      Boston, Mass. 02111
   381 Dorchester Street
      So. Boston, Mass. 02127
   325 Main Street
      Fitchburg, Mass. 01420

In New York
   78 Fort Place
      Staten Island, N.Y. 10301
   625 East 187th Street
      Bronx, N.Y. 10458
   525 Main Street
      Buffalo, N.Y. 14203

In Connecticut
   202 Fairfield Avenue
      Bridgeport, Conn. 06603

In Ohio
   415 Euclid Avenue
      Cleveland, Ohio 44114

In Pennsylvania
   1127 South Broad Street
      Philadelphia, Pa. 19147

In Florida
   2700 Biscayne Blvd.
      Miami, Florida 33137

In Lousiana
   331 Harrison Ave.
      New Orleans, La. 70124
   86 Bolton Avenue
      Alexandria, La. 71301

In Texas
   114 East Main Plaza
      San Antonio, Texas 78205

In California
   1570 Fifth Avenue
      San Diego, Calif. 92101
   278 - 17th Street
      Oakland, Calif. 94612

In Canada
   8885 Blvd. Lacordaire
   St. Leonard Deport-Maurice
      Montreal, Canada
   1063 St. Clair Avenue West
      Toronto, Canada

In Australia
   58 Abbotsford Road
      Homebush, N.S.W.,
      2140 Sydney, Australia

In Africa
   20, Kampala and 3A. Vioram St.
      Kampala, Uganda

In England
   57, Kensington Church St.
      London, W. 8, England

In India
   143, Water Field Road
      Bandra
      Bombay 50-AS, India

In Philippine Islands
   2650, B.B. Harrison
   P.O. Box 3576
      Pasay City, Philippine Islands

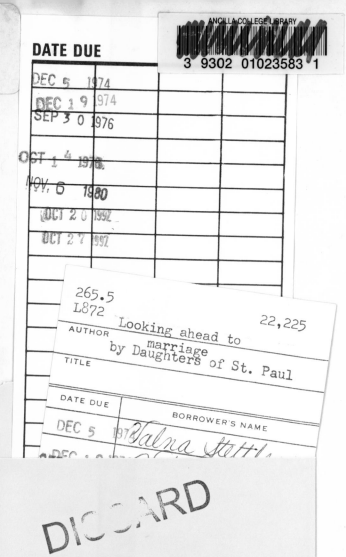